China-Mongolia Economic Corridor

Modern China Series

China-Mongolia Economic Corridor

Research on Social Responsibility of Resource-oriented Enterprises

Eerdun Taoketao

Zhang Zhe

Wang Gang

Wei Lisi

North American Business Press

CHINA-MONGOLIA ECONOMIC CORRIDOR

ISBN 978-1-948915-09-0

North American Business Press
Atlanta, Georgia
Miami, Florida
New York, New York,
Toronto, Canada

FIRST PRINTING, 2019

About Modern China Series

China, as one of the oldest civilized regions in the world, has emerged as something of a "new world" because it is working to embrace its own essence and heritage and link them to viable economic strategies. In the last 25 years, China has made tremendous strides by doing so. The country and her people have every right to take pride in these accomplishments. With these successes under their belt, many Chinese leaders and intellectuals anticipate continuing growth. China's plans and strategies, furthermore, are often based upon this premise.

There is tremendous interest in the US on the Chinese economy and business environment. China has emerged as a global super power, and scholars and businessmen in the US are keenly interested in learning how this is going to continue to affect them and how they can do business with China. In response to growing interest from international and Asian scholars, North American Business Press is pleased to announce our Modern China Series (MCS) books, which is first of such series in the US and has garnered tremendous interest both in the US and around the world. With our first book reaching stores in September 2011, this initiative is aimed at developing relationships between NABP and Chinese scholars who desire to promote their academic and applied business writings to the rest of the world.

We have had overwhelming demand for the Modern China Series from both authors who would like to publish in the series and people who would like to read the books. Currently, there are ten books published in the series and, additionally, we have a couple of dozen books that we are considering for the series. The books have been viewed by tens of thousands of people from the U. S. and the rest of the world.

We have published books relating to several areas revolving around the Chinese business environment. We have a few that focus on the best practices in marketing in China; a couple relating to "best practices" in doing business in China; and a few on the outlook of the Chinese economy. The market for the Modern China Series is huge. There are tens of thousands of scholars that are keenly interested in the continued growth of the Chinese economy and the implications that will have on the business world. Even more significant are the millions of businessmen that are interested in the impact that China will continue to have on the global economy. It is difficult to pin down the exact demand for the series, but it Is very large.

We have big plans for growing the Moderns China Series. This has the potential to one of the most significant economic/business series ever produced. We are very selective with the books that we will add to the collection, but we encourage any scholars who think they have unique and interesting perspectives on China to submit their books to us. From the readers perspective, we are committed to producing high quality books on a regular basis so that readers should expect a steady stream of insightful books to be coming out for many years to come.

This initiative is headed by Dr. Robert Tian, a renowned researcher and academic, who spearheads our efforts in partnering with foreign authors and administering day-to-day operations of this series. Dr. Tian, a Vice-President with North American Business Press and Editor of this series, spends much of his time in Beijing, Shanghai, and other Chinese cities, focusing on developing and managing our interests with authors and universities. Below is the list for the books we have published:

Enterprise Strategy: New Horizon authored by Zhang Xiuyu
Governance of Private Enterprises in Modern China authored by Zhong Qin
The Art of War and Enterprise Strategy Management authored by Fu Shouzhi
Marketing Issues in Modern China edited by Robert Guang Tian et al.
The Footprints of the Academician authored by Fu Zhouzhi

Marketing and Economics in Modern China (I) edited by Xiaoguang Qi et al.

Marketing and Economics in Modern China (II) edited by Wang Tianjin et al.

An Islamic Heritage in China authored by Ma Zhanming

China Environmental Anthropology authored by Wang Tianjin, Tian Guang, and Ma Jianfu

Can China Rule the New World? Authored by Tian Guang and Chen Gang

Critiques on Pan-Marketization authored by Li Cunlin, Liu Hongfei, and Tian Guang

Economic and Business Anthropology in China edited by Xiaoguang Qi and Tian Guang

China-Mongolia Economic Corridor authored by Eerdun Taoketao, Zhang Zhe, Wang Gang and Wei Lisi

Preface

In September 2016, Outline of the Plan on Establishing the China-Mongolia-Russia Economic Corridor was released, opening a new chapter for cooperation between China, Mongolia and Russia under the framework of the Belt and Road Initiative. Mongolia is in the middle of the China-Mongolia-Russia Economic Corridor and is a key pivot point of the northern line of the Belt and Road. China and Mongolia are both important producers of mineral resources with mining industry in the world, and then exploitation of mineral resources is one of the important fields of China-Mongolia economic and trade cooperation. Mongolia is rich in resources but lacking in capital and technology, while China has sufficient capital, technology and market, which complements Mongolia in industry. At present, 67.3% of China's investment capital in Mongolia is concentrated in the fields of geology and mining (Yu, 2015). With the construction and development of the China-Mongolia Economic Corridor in depth and breadth, it will be of extensive prospects for the development of China and Mongolia to take advantage of the adjacent advantages between the two countries, to realize their economic and social benefits in the exploitation and cooperation of resources.

In the context of the China-Mongolia Economic Corridor, resource-based enterprises have more opportunities available, and the increase in resources imports and exports will enable relevant enterprises to take advantage of such opportunities to achieve sustainable development, while driving the development of national and local economy. However, the increase of trading volume and the development of regional economy should not be carried out at the cost of the deterioration of ecological environment. Especially for resource-based enterprises, their own features determine the necessity of fulfilling their own social responsibilities. However, in real life, there is an evident lack of social responsibility among resource-based enterprises. Based on the strategic thinking of building a community with shared interests, shared responsibilities and a shared future in the Belt and Road Initiative, China must actively promote the social responsibility movement of resource-based enterprises, which can not only improve the image of such enterprises in the public and enhance their capacity for sustainable development. Moreover, the positive fulfillment of social responsibility by resource-based enterprises in China can protect the ecological and social environment of the surrounding areas of the "China-Mongolia-Russia Economic Corridor" and contribute to maintaining regional and national stability and building a community with a shared future for mankind.

Research on the advancement of social responsibility of resource-based enterprises is not only a problem of enterprises themselves, but also a global social problem. Therefore, it has been unable to adapt to the current status of economic development and globalization by studying corporate social responsibility from a single point of view. Under the framework of "the China-Mongolia Economic Corridor", this paper explores the strategy and mechanism of the coordinated advancement of the social responsibility of resource-based enterprises in China and Mongolia, and clarifies the stakeholders in the coordinated advancement of social responsibility, establishes a reasonable and effective mechanism for the coordinated governance of stakeholders, serves the common interests of China and Mongolia and thus boosts the sustainable development of the China-Mongolia Economic Corridor and stability and unity in border areas. Based on the above research background and significance, this book mainly studies the following aspects:

First, the current status and reasons for the performance of social responsibility are analyzed against the resource-based enterprises along the China-Mongolia Economic Corridor. The development of resources shows the characteristics of multi-objective, multi-subject, multi-level and multi-function complex relations. The social responsibility involved in the process of resource development by resource-based enterprises can be divided into three subsystems of economy, nature and society. In this regard, this paper investigates the status quo of the resource-based enterprises of China-Mongolia Economic Corridor and that of the performance of their social responsibility in the China-Mongolia cooperative development from three aspects of economy, nature and society, and analyses the problems and reasons in the performance of corporate social responsibility.

Second, the subjects for the coordinated advancement of social responsibility of the resource-based enterprises along the China-Mongolia Economic Corridor are clarified and determined, and the coordinated advancement model for corporate social responsibility is established. In the context of the China-Mongolia Economic Corridor, this study clarifies the subjects for the coordinated advancement of corporate social responsibility in accordance with the particularity of social responsibility of transnational resource-based enterprises and the close relationship between resource development and stakeholders and the significance of stakeholders' impact. From the perspective of coordination, the mechanism for the coordinated advancement of social responsibility is established for the transnational resource-based enterprises along the China-Mongolia Economic Corridor, for mobilizing people from all walks of life in China and Mongolia to jointly promote the realization of corporate social responsibility.

Third, the formation and implementation for the coordinated advancement mechanism of social responsibility of the resource-based enterprises along the China-Mongolia Economic Corridor are studied. The coordinated advancement mechanism of corporate social responsibility is neither a simple combination nor a product naturally formed, but arises in the process that the subjects carry out purposeful, reasonable and orderly actions under the guidance of the concept of coordinated advancement of corporate social responsibility, on the premise of fully understanding their own responsibilities and conditions, so as to realize the optimization of corporate social responsibility, the dynamic and balanced development of economic, social and ecological benefits. The goal of the coordinated advancement mechanism is to implement the coordinated advancement mechanism of corporate social responsibility to the actual operational level of each subject, which is the key step to achieve the synergistic effect. This study puts forward specific measures for the implementation of the mechanism from three aspects of formation mechanism, implementation mechanism and evaluation mechanism.

Fourth, some policy suggestions are given for the coordinated advancement mechanism of social responsibility of the resource-based enterprises along the China-Mongolia Economic Corridor. The implementation of the coordinated advancement mechanism of social responsibility of transnational resource-based enterprises along the China-Mongolia Economic Corridor is a global issue, which requires the interaction and cooperation of enterprises, governments and society. This study puts forward corresponding countermeasures for the subjects concerning the coordinated advancement mechanism of corporate social responsibility, thus contributing to the harmonious and win-win development of the China-Mongolia Economic Corridor.

The innovation in this study is that, through literature review, the authors have found scholars at home and abroad have gradually paid pay attention to the issue of social responsibility in cross-border economic cooperation under the Belt and Road Initiative, but there are few studies on social responsibility of resource-based enterprises in cross-border economic cooperation. Furthermore, the previous studies on social responsibility of resource-based enterprises are all carried out from the perspective of how enterprises fulfill their social responsibility in their own country or region, and no studies focus on the transnational coordinated advancement mechanism from the perspective of coordinated development of regional economy and society. The research on China-Mongolia cooperation is mainly based on the cooperative development of resources and the protection of ecological environment, while the research and practice of coordinated advancement of social responsibility fulfillment of resource-based enterprises in the two countries are seldom involved.

Taking the Belt and Road Initiative as the breakthrough point and the resource-based enterprises of the China-Mongolia Economic

Corridor as the research object, this paper studies the social responsibility fulfillment of the resource-based enterprises of the China-Mongolia Economic Corridor from the perspectives of the ecological environment sharing of China and Mongolia and the sustainable economic development of the China-Mongolia Economic Corridor and the approaches to the implementation of the coordinated advancement of social responsibility of resource-based enterprises in the two countries.

The book is based on the research topic of the State Ethnic Affairs Commission of the People's Republic of China, and is co-authored by Professor Eerdun Taoketao, Associate Professor Zhang Zhe and Associate Professor Wang Gang of Inner Mongolia University of Finance and Economics, China. Most of the writers have doctoral degrees and rich research experience, with many theoretical studies and practice surveys into resource-based enterprises in China and Mongolia. It is hoped that the findings of this study can serve the common interests of China and Mongolia and promote the sustainable development of the China-Mongolia Economic Corridor and the stability and unity of the border areas, providing some references for the construction of other cross-border economic cooperation zones.

Acknowledgements

Based on the Belt and Road Initiative in China, there have been many problems arising from the rapid development of the China-Mongolia-Russia Economic Corridor, among which the trans-regional corporate social responsibility is a crucial issue affecting the sustainable development of enterprises and countries, and urgently needs the attention of academic circles and business circles. In this context, our research group applied for the topic titled Research on Coordinated Advancement Mechanism of Social Responsibilities of Resource-based Enterprises in the China-Mongolia Economic Corridor and completed it after more than two years of investigation and research. This monograph is based on the research topic as the product of the collective wisdom of our research group. In the past two years, the members of the research group have read a lot of relevant literature, visited many resource-based enterprises in China and Mongolia, and devoted ourselves to writing a scientific and practical research report. As the monograph is about to be published, we would like to express our heartfelt gratitude to all our friends and colleagues who have supported and helped us. First of all, we are greatly indebted to the State Ethnic Affairs Commission of the People's Republic of China which financed our project. With the support of the national government, we would be able to conduct in-depth research on this issue. Secondly, we would also like to acknowledge our indebtedness to all the members of our research group, especially Yi Ruhan and Caolumen Qiqige, and the graduate students Sun Na, Gu Qidi, Fang Jijing, Zhao Min, Zhao Ying among many others, who are mostly college teachers and can take time off to participate in the discussion, research and writing of the project on the premise of their onerous teaching and research tasks. Their rigorous and earnest working attitude guarantees the scientific nature of our research results. Finally, we would like to owe a special debt of gratitude to the unknown staff who translated, proofread and contacted the publishing house for us when preparing to publish the monograph. Without their hard work, it would be impossible for us to publish our research findings abroad and communicate with foreign scholars in academic studies! In addition, our gratitude also extends to our family members and friends for their contributions without complaints when we prepare to publish the monograph. In the future life and study, we will pay back to our motherland and relatives with more outstanding research findings!

Foreword

Robert Guang Tian

Since Chinese President Xi Jinping put forward the Belt and Road Initiative in 2013, great achievements have been made in the building of the Belt and Road, and the countries have negotiated with each other concerning cooperative construction and sharing. At present, more than 100 countries and international organizations have participated in the Initiative, and the building of the Belt and Road is also included in the important resolutions adopted by the UN General Assembly and the UN Security Council. Under the strategic concept of the Belt and Road, President Xi Jinping proposed an initiative of building the China-Mongolia-Russia Economic Corridor at the meeting of the heads of state of China, Mongolia and Russia in September 2014, which aims to connect the Trans-Eurasian Railway of Russia and the Development Road of Mongolia, and get through the economic cooperation corridor between the three countries based on the links of transportation, freight transportation and transnational power grids. The China- Mongolia-Russia Economic Corridor is a supplement and expansion to the Belt and Road Initiative, and forms a whole with the Belt and Road Initiative, which means that the strategy of the Silk Road Economic Belt has expanded from the development mode of cooperation between China and Central Asia mainly based on the Eurasian Continental Bridge to that of cooperation between China and Russia, Mongolia on the northeast. On July 9, 2015, the heads of state of China, Mongolia and Russia met in Ufa, Russia, reaching consensus on the principles, directions and key areas of in-depth tripartite cooperation. During the meeting, it was decided that China's Silk Road Economic Belt, Russia's Trans-Eurasian Corridor and Mongolia's Development Road would be connected to promote the construction of the China-Mongolia-Russia Economic Corridor.

On June 23, 2016, Chinese President Xi Jinping, Russia President Vladimir Putin and Mongolian President Tsakhiagiin Elbegdorj held the third meeting in Tashi and signed the Outline of the Plan on Establishing the China-Mongolia-Russia Economic Corridor, which further enhances the close ties between China, Mongolia and Russia by increasing the volume of tripartite trade, enhancing product competitiveness, strengthening the interconnectivity of railways and highways, facilitating customs clearance and transport, and boosting transit transport cooperation, studying the construction of tripartite cross-border transmission networks, carrying out practical cooperation in tourism, think tanks, media, environmental protection, disaster reduction and relief and other fields. With the in-depth development of the China-Mongolia Economic Corridor, resource-based enterprises have more opportunities available, and the increase in resources imports and exports will enable relevant enterprises to take advantage of such opportunities to achieve sustainable development, while driving the development of national and local economy. However, the increase of trading volume and the development of regional economy should not be carried out at the cost of the deterioration of ecological environment. Especially for resource-based enterprises, their own features determine the necessity of fulfilling their own social responsibilities. However, in real life, there is an evident lack of social responsibility among resource-based enterprises, which arouses several environmental and social problems, and is not conducive to the rapid development of the China-Mongolia Economic Corridor.

Based on the above international background, this monograph studies the social responsibility of transnational resource-based enterprises in the China-Mongolia Economic Corridor. This book analyzes the social responsibility of trans-regional and transnational enterprises from a coordinated point of view, which not only enriches and develops the theory of corporate social responsibility and geo-economic theory, but also promotes the sustainable development of the China-Mongolia Economic Corridor and the stability and unity of border areas. The key features of this monograph are as follows:

Innovation in research fields: Corporate social responsibility has a bearing on the sustainable development of enterprises and countries, so scholars at home and abroad pay more attention to social responsibility. However, the focus of the study is on the social responsibility in the region, and there are few studies on social responsibility of trans-regional and even transnational enterprises. Especially for the construction of "the China-Mongolia Economic Corridor", its goal and direction is trans-regional cooperation and win-win result. In this regard, the book can study cross-regional corporate social responsibility, which reflects the innovation of research fields.

Innovation in research perspective: Trans-regional corporate social responsibility should be confronted with several stakeholders, and each stakeholder belongs to different institutions and countries, and thus there will be more complex problems. Therefore, it is not operable to study cross-regional corporate social responsibility from a single perspective. This book studies cross-regional corporate social responsibility from the perspective of coordination, carries out coordination and supervision on the fulfillment of corporate social responsibility from the overall perspective, which will be of greater practical significance, and offer new perspectives and approaches for the solution to trans-regional problems.

Based on long-term theoretical accumulation and regional and ethnic advantages, the authors of the book have conducted many field surveys on resource-based enterprises in China and Mongolia, obtained abundant and detailed first-hand data, and developed theoretical and practical research findings, thereby contributing to the economic development of ethnic regions in China. It is hoped that more capable and talented scholars will be concerned about economic management in ethnic regions in China and make contributions to creating a harmonious and win-win result!

Table of Contents

Chapter 1

Introduction

1.1 Research Background and Significance

1.1.1 Research Background

At present, the world is in the period of great development, momentous change and great adjustment. Peace and development are still the theme of the times. The world multi-polarization, economic globalization and cultural diversity are developing in depth. The global governance system and reform of the international order have accelerated, and countries have become increasingly interconnected and dependent. At the same time, the world faces uncertainties in instability, the world's economic growth momentum is insufficient, the polarization between the rich and the poor is growing, regional hotspots are on the rise, and non-traditional security threats such as terrorism, cyber security, major communicable diseases, and climate change continue to spread. Humanity faces many familiar challenges. Based on deep thinking about history and reality, in the fall of 2013, Chinese president Xi Jinping proposed "the Belt and Road". Over the past four years, the construction of "the Belt and Road" has made great progress and has formed a cooperation situation in which all countries have jointly built. At present, more than 100 countries and international organizations have participated in it, and important resolutions such as the UN General Assembly and the UN Security Council have also been included in the program construction. "The Belt and Road" construction highlights the top-level design, and the "Vision and Action for Promoting the Silk Road Economic Belt and the 21st Century Maritime Silk Road" document, issued in March 2015, has put forward the design framework of "Belt and Road", from the main principle, main line and direction of construction.

Under the strategic concept of "the Belt and Road", in September 2014, when President Xi Jinping attended the meeting of the heads of state of China, Russia and Mongolia, he proposed the China-Mongolia-Russia economic corridor construction initiative, that is, the joint of Russian Trans-Eurasian Railway and the Mongolian "Prairie Road" will be carried out to link the three countries' economic cooperation corridors with transportation, cargo transportation and cross-border power grids. The "China-Mongolia-Russia Economic Corridor" complements and expands "the Belt and Road" concept and forms a whole with the strategic concept. This means that the "Silk Road Economic Belt" strategy, which has mainly relied on the Asia-Europe Continental Bridge to develop cooperation between China and Central Asia, has developed to expand to the Northeast to cooperate with China and Russia.

On July 9, 2015, the heads of state of China, Mongolia and Russia met in Ufa, Russia, to reach the principles, directions and key areas of deep cooperation between the three parties. During the meeting, it was decided to link China's Silk Road economic belt construction, Russia's trans-Eurasian channel construction, and Mongolia's "Prairie Road" to promote the construction of China-Mongolia-Russia economic corridor. On June 23, 2016, Chinese President Xi Jinping, Russian President Vladimir Putin and Mongolian President Elbegdorj held a third meeting between the heads of state of China, Mongolia and Russia in Tash, and signed *the Outline of the Plan for the Construction of China-Russia Economic* Corridor. It says by increasing the tripartite trade, to promote the competitiveness of the products, to strengthen the construction of railways, highways and other connectivity, to promote the customs clearance and transport facilitation, to promote cooperation transit transport, the tripartite cross-border grid construction, to develop tourism, think tanks, media, pragmatic cooperation in areas such as environmental protection, disaster reduction and relief, and to further strengthen the close contact of the three sides. The three parties can deepen cooperation within the framework of the Shanghai Cooperation Organization to jointly safeguard regional security and achieve common development.

Resources-oriented Enterprise is a type of enterprise that is different from manufacturing enterprises, technology-based enterprises, and service-oriented enterprise, in terms of labor-intensive, capital-intensive, technology-intensive, and knowledge-intensive. It refers to the possession or monopoly (quantity and cost) of natural resources (mainly underground mineral resources and aboveground plant and animal resources), taking the exploitation of natural resources and primary processing as the basic production mode, relying on the resource consumption to achieve enterprise growth, and treating resource dominance as the core competitiveness (Jia, 2008). Such enterprises can be divided into coal mining industry, oil and gas exploration industry, non-ferrous metal mining industry, non-metallic mineral mining industry and timber harvesting industry according to resource types (Ji, 2009).

In 2002, there were 6,977 state-owned and above-scale non-state-owned resource-oriented industrial enterprises, of which 40.5% were distributed in the coal industry, 24.5% in the non-metallic mining industry, 18.5% in the non-ferrous metal mining industry, and 10% in the non-ferrous metal mining industry. In the ferrous metal mining industry, 5.5% are engaged in timber harvesting, and the oil and gas mining industry accounts for only 1.2% of resource-oriented enterprises. In September 2016, the *Planning Outline of China-Mongolia-Russia Economic Corridor* was released, which opened a new chapter in the cooperation between China, Mongolia and Russia under the framework of "the Belt and Road". Among them, Mongolia is in the middle of the Corridor and is an important fulcrum of "the Belt and Road" North Line.

China and Mongolia are both important mining countries in the world. Mineral resources development is one of the major areas of China-Mongolia economic and trade cooperation. Mongolia has state-owned resources, lacks funds, lacks technology, and China has funds, technology, and market, which forms a complementary industry with Mongolia. At present, 67.3% of China's investment capital in Mongolia is concentrated in the field of geology and mining (Yu, 2015). With the in-depth development of the "China-Mongolia Economic Corridor" (CMEC), it has broad prospects for development by taking advantage of the adjoining advantages between China and Mongolia, to achieve mutual economic and social benefits in the exploitation and cooperation of resource. In macro context of CMEC, more opportunities are brought to resource-oriented enterprises. The increase in the import and export trade of resources will enable related enterprises to take advantage of good opportunities to achieve sustainable development, while promoting the development of national and local economies. However, the increase in trade volume and the development of the local economy cannot be at the expense of the deterioration of the ecological environment. Especially for resource-oriented enterprises, their own characteristics determine the necessity of enterprises to fulfill their social responsibilities.

In real life, the phenomenon of the lack of social responsibility of resource-oriented enterprises is extremely obvious. Resource-oriented enterprises use non-renewable resources for development, and many cities in China have been included in the ranks of depleted resources and urban industrial transformation. Due to the limitation of technology level, the constraints of capital, equipment and talents, resource-oriented enterprises have extensive mining methods, and the waste of resources caused by indiscriminate mining is prominent. The cost of high efficiency and high growth is high input of exploitation resources, high energy consumption and high waste discharge. For example, most of the Inner Mongolia coal mining areas are in the living areas of Mongolian farmers. The mining area collapse caused by unreasonable coal mining, grassland destruction, and the "three wastes" problem have seriously affected the lives of residents and caused prohibitive costs for the whole society. In addition, the frequent occurrence of mine accidents also reflects the weak sense of resource-oriented Corporate Social Responsibility (CSR). Mine accidents not only widen the gap between the rich and the poor, but also easily intensify some social contradictions and threaten the stability and unity of society. Problems such as low wages of employees, poor working environment, and lack of protection of legitimate rights and interests have also become a severe injury to resource-oriented enterprises.

In order to build a community of interests, a community of destiny and a community of responsibility, China must actively promote the resource-oriented CSR movement. One the one side, it helps improve the image of resource-oriented enterprises in the public mind, enhance the sustainable development capability of enterprises, avoid the detours and problems encountered by developed countries, avoid the irreparable damage to the natural environment while developing economy. On the other side, it helps alleviate the conflict between labor and capital of enterprises, protect the economic rights and interests of the country and the people, and promote the sustainable development of the national economy. What's more, China's resource-oriented enterprises can actively fulfill their social responsibilities to protect the ecological and social environment of surrounding areas of the China-Mongolia-Russia Economic Corridor and contribute to maintaining regional and national stability and building a community with shared future for humanity.

In conclusion, from the macro perspective of the international political and economic situation, to build a harmonious society and realize the Chinese dream of peace, development, cooperation and win-win model, resource-oriented enterprises must consciously perform corporate social responsibilities. From the microscopic point of view, the problems arising from the development of resource-oriented enterprises in China are the requirements of CSR in economic, legal, environmental protection and ethics. Only enterprises that actively fulfill their social responsibilities can ultimately obtain the support of customers, consumers, the public, the government and the society, gain a good reputation, establish a good corporate image, and thus gain long-term advantages in grasping market information, acquiring superior resources, and winning customers, and finally achieve sustainable company development. Therefore, promoting the fulfillment of CSR in resource-oriented enterprises has a broad and profound realistic background.

1.1.2 Research Significance

This project is based on the international background of the construction of the CMEC. It is of great significance both in terms of theoretical value and practical value, which is mainly reflected in the following two aspects:

First, from the perspective of theoretical value, the study of the promotion of resource-oriented enterprise social responsibility is not only a problem of the enterprise itself, but a global social problem. From the existing research literature on CSR, most of the theoretical research and practical exploration of CSR are based on the single perspective of the government and society overlooking enterprises, and the interaction between enterprises, government and society is insufficient. Especially in the construction of CMEC, the behavior of a certain enterprise not only has an impact on itself but is more likely to have an enormous impact on its region, country and other regions and countries involved in the enterprise. Therefore, the study of CSR from a single perspective can hardly adapt to the current economic development and internationalization background. Under the framework of CMEC, this project discusses the strategies and mechanisms of synergy of social responsibility of resource-oriented enterprises in China-Mongolia, defines the stakeholders in the implementation of coordinated promotion of social responsibility, enriches and develops the theories of CSR and geo-economic.

Second, from the perspective of practical value, the construction of social responsibility coordination mechanism of resource-oriented enterprises in CMEC provides a good reference value and reference for the construction of other cross-border economic cooperation zones. At present, there are more than 6,000 Chinese companies in Mongolia. With China's growing domestic energy and resource cravings, the development of Mongolian minerals and other resources will further increase, which will inevitably lead to ecological problems such as environmental pollution. However, the regional ecological environment in China, which is adjacent to Mongolia, is not optimistic. China and Mongolia are dependent on each other, realizing the sharing of ecological environment is an important environmental guarantee for the sustainable development of the CMEC. On the other hand, if Mongolian resource-oriented enterprises neglect the fulfillment of social responsibilities, they will inevitably cause ecological risks and other social problems, damage the image and reputation of Chinese enterprises, and bring certain difficulties to Chinese enterprises to continue to develop Mongolian mineral resources. It will cast a shadow over the long-term stable development of the CMEC. Therefore, the sustainable development of CMEC calls for resource-oriented enterprises to assume social responsibilities. This project will establish a reasonable and effective stakeholder synergy mechanism, to serve the common interests of China and Mongolia, and promote the sustainable development of the CMEC and the stable and united frontier regions. The construction of the social responsibility coordination mechanism of resource-oriented enterprises in the CMEC has reference value for the construction of other cross-border economic cooperation zones.

1.2 Research Design, Methods, Content and Major Innovations

1.2.1 Research Design

First, through field research and interviews, understand the status quo of social responsibility fulfillment of resource-oriented enterprises in the CMEC, and analyze the problems and causes in the process of fulfilling CSR to establish the necessity of research. Second, based on previous field research and interviews, the main body of the coordinated promotion of social responsibility of resource-oriented enterprises in the CMEC is established, and a dynamic game model is constructed, which lays a foundation for the formation and implementation of the follow-up resource-oriented CSR coordination promotion mechanism. Third, from the three parts of formation, implementation and evaluation, the specific implementation process of the coordinated promotion mechanism of social responsibility of China-Mongolia transnational resource-oriented enterprises is comprehensively expounded. Fourth, from the perspective of cooperation, this research proposes countermeasures and suggestions on the coordinated promotion of social responsibility of transnational resource-oriented enterprises in the economic corridor of China and Mongolia.

1.2.2 Research Methods

1. Literature analysis method

By collecting various media information and policy documents, the relevant research and practice results are sorted out and reviewed, which provides the basis for subsequent field investigations and interviews.

2. Field investigation method

Based on literature research, through field investigations, visiting the resource-oriented enterprises of the CMEC, the relevant administrative departments of the Chinese and Mongolian governments, the social management departments of the enterprises, residents and farmers and herdsmen, to obtain first-hand data.

3. Case analysis method

Through the case introduction of the social responsibility coordinated promotion practice of the typical resource-oriented enterprises in the CMEC, it is found that there is still room for improvement and improvement in the current synergy process.

4. Game evolution method

Based on the perspective of stakeholder theory, the game evolution method is used to dynamically deduct the behavior of resource-oriented CSR stakeholders and construct a synergistic mechanism.

1.2.3 Research Content

1. Status quo of social responsibility implementation of resource-oriented enterprises.

The resources development shows characteristics of multi-objective, multi-subject, multi-level, multi-functional complex relationship. The social responsibility involved in the resource-oriented enterprise resource development process can be mainly subdivided into three subsystems: economic, natural and social. Therefore, this research mainly analyzes the status quo of social responsibility fulfillment of resource-oriented enterprises in CMEC and cooperative development from aspects of economy, nature and society, as well as the existing problems and causes of CSR fulfillment.

2. Clear out and clarify the main body of the coordinated promotion of social responsibility of resource-oriented enterprises in the CMEC and construct a dynamic game model between subjects.

This research does not lay in the solution of specific social responsibility issues, but from a macroscopic perspective, through the establishment of a mechanism for the coordinated promotion of CSR, mobilize the forces from all walks of life in China and Mongolia to jointly promote the realization of CSR. It combines the particularity of resource-oriented CSR and confirms the main body of CSR synergy based on the close relationship between resource development and various stakeholders and the importance of stakeholder influence. Furthermore, through the game model, it is possible to realize the maximization of the overall benefits of the three subsystems of economy, nature and society under the conditions of the collaborative propulsion subject.

3. The formation and implementation of the social responsibility coordination promotion mechanism for resource-oriented enterprises in the CMEC.

The formation of the CSR coordination promotion mechanism is not a simple unity, nor will it be formed naturally. It is a purposeful, reasonable and orderly course of action conducted by each subject, based on fully understanding their own responsibility and conditions and under the guidance of jointly promoting the concept of CSR, to optimize CSR, economic benefits, social benefits and ecological benefits of dynamic balanced development. The goal of the synergy mechanism is to implement the cooperative promotion mechanism of CSR into the actual operation level of each subject. This research will propose specific implementation measures and recommendations from three aspects, respectively formation mechanism, implementation mechanism and evaluation mechanism.

1.2.4 Major Innovations

At present, many scholars have studied the opportunities, challenges, cooperation methods and policies of economic and trade cooperation between China and Mongolia from the perspectives of economic development, political relations, trade issues and resource cooperation (EEnkhtaivan, 2016;Batqiqige, 2014;Betsuhe, 2014; Xie, 2017;Liu, 2016).

In the research on bilateral cooperation in field of resources cooperation, the research has gradually expanded from cooperation mechanism, infrastructure and mutual trust to eco-environmental protection mechanism construction and environmental risks (Zhang, 2005; Jiang, Zhang, 2012; Pu and Li, 2016). This also shows that scholars are gradually paying attention to the issue of social responsibility in cross-border economic cooperation. However, there are still relatively few relevant literatures on resource-oriented CSR in cross-border economic cooperation. Moreover, in the past, the research on resource-oriented CSR is based on how the enterprise fulfills its social responsibility in one country or one region and does not conduct cross-country coordinated research from the perspective of regional economic and social coordinated development.

On the research of China-Mongolia cooperation, it is mainly carried out from the perspectives of resource cooperation development and ecological environment protection. The research and practice of cooperation between the two parties to promote the fulfillment of social responsibility of resource-oriented enterprises is hardly involved. This project is based on "the Belt and Road" strategy and takes resource-oriented enterprises of CMEC as the research object. From the perspective of ecological environment sharing in central Mongolia and the sustainable development of CMEC, it discusses the fulfillment of social responsibility of resource-oriented enterprises in the CMEC, as well as how China and Mongolia can jointly promote the implementation of social responsibility of resource-oriented enterprises. This is the innovation of this project.

Chapter 2

Theoretical Bases and Research Status

2.1 Concept Definition of Corporate Social Responsibility

In the process of CSR development, the definition and paradigm structure of CSR has been widely controversial (Bowen, 1953; Carroll, 1979; Clarkson, 1995; Brown and Dacin, 1997; Carroll, 1999). It is difficult to define CSR, but it does not mean that it cannot be defined (Marrewijk, 2003). The definition of CSR ranges from requiring active ethical practice to requiring companies to improve social welfare, so that CSR is considered an empty definition by some people, while some others believe that all the definitions of CSR are appropriate as these definitions are all based on the interests of different stakeholders in the company. As American jurist Manne (1972) puts it, the most fashionable concept of CSR has not yet formed a unified, generally accepted concept. However, it should be acknowledged that it is precisely because of this ambiguity that CSR has been widely supported (Ston, 1975). With the development of CSR theory and practice, the ambiguity of its concept has increasingly become an obstacle to its development.

Defining corporate social responsibility is of great significance. First, Carroll (1999), through a review of all the definitions of CSR from the 1950s to the 1990s, pointed out that all of these definitions can be modified and improved, but a clear, universal concept has not yet been proposed. After six years of Carroll's work, Dahlsrud (2008) tried to define CSR, but he encountered the same problem as Carroll, that is, the current definition lacks wide applicability. Second, an in-depth understanding of corporate social responsibility can contribute to the development of CSR theory and practice. Third, the research trends defining CSR continue to expand, especially in developing countries. This is mainly because CSR is currently in the stage of rapid development in developing countries. However, the definition of CSR is usually regarded as abstract, without breakthrough theoretical development and practical research.

The definition of CSR was formed in many years of theoretical and practical research, especially in developed and industrialized countries such as the United Kingdom, other countries in Europe, and the United States. Howard Bowen (1953) was one of the first scholars to define CSR, and his early definitions still have an important impact on today's research on CSR theory and practice. He believes that corporate decision-making not only affects the behavior of the company itself, but also affects the entire society. According to his view, the purpose of corporate social responsibility is not to solve specific business and social problems, but to serve as an effective mechanism to assist the development of the company. Howard Bowen is called "the father of corporate social responsibility" (Carroll, 1999).

In the 1960s, the definitions of CSR increased rapidly. Davis (1960) considers that the influence of entrepreneurs can promote the development of corporate social responsibility. Frederick (1960) proposed that corporate social responsibility is an expectation of society, and McGuire (1963) argues that corporate social responsibility puts higher demands on enterprises and exceeds half of the requirements of the economy and society. The European Commission believes that act of establishing social responsibility policies to solve environmental problems is based on the resources of the company's own business operations and stakeholders. Based on this view, corporate social responsibility is not only the implementation of the law, and more investment in human capital, the environment, and stakeholder relationships are required (Walton, 1964). These scholars all recognize that the relationship between business and society is an important part of CSR.

Later, in the 1970s, researches on the CSR definitions made great progress. More specific definitions were made during that time. Johnson (1971), Davis (1960), Steiner (1971), Eells and Walton (1974), Sethi (1975), Preston and Post (1975) and Carroll (1999) argue that corporate social responsibility is related to ethics, economic interests, stakeholders and social obligations. For example, according to Johnson (1971), if a company has a sense of social responsibility, it must consider the interests of employees, suppliers, dealers, local communities and the country. Corporate social responsibility is more an attitude, that is, the attitude of an organization to help society achieve its basic goals. Other scholars consider that corporate social responsibility is not just about creating profits (Davis, 1960; Backman, 1975), it is a spontaneous behavior that transcends the economic requirements of the law (Manne and Wallich, 1972), a concern for society (Eells and Walton, 1961), and a method of social response (Sethi, 1975; Ackerman and Bauer, 1976). Then, some researches on CSR focus on economic issues and the pressure of interest groups (Marens, 2008).

In the 1980s, the focus of CSR research was shifted to corporate ethics. During the 80s and 90s, research on the concept of CSR had been reduced. Although there were many related publications currently, the concept of CSR was still not clear enough (Clarkson, 1995). The main research trend currently was the alternative concepts and subjects. Relevant concepts and theories such as corporate social responsibility performance, corporate social response, business ethics and stakeholders were developed. Most of the research work then began to shift to the operational research of corporate social responsibility.

In the 21st century, corporate social responsibility has reflected the trend of globalization in both theoretical and practical research, and corporate social responsibility has become a global issue. Social marketing is a new beginning in the study of CSR at this time. Kotleretal (2005) pointed out that in the concept of social marketing, marketers must balance three aspects when formulating marketing strategies: corporate profits, consumers' desire and social interests. At the same time, the research on social responsibility of supply chain enterprises has begun to rise. The view is that corporate social responsibility is no longer the social responsibility decision-making and management of individual enterprises, nor is it aimed at solving a social problem, corporate social responsibility is closely related to the entire supply chain.

Table 2.1 lists the representative definitions of corporate social responsibility from the 1960s to the present.

Table 2.1 Definitions of Representative Corporate Social Responsibility

Time	Author	Definition
1960	Davis	This theory holds that corporate social responsibility corresponds to the rights of merchants.
1960	Frederick	Social responsibility means an economic operating system in which merchants meet public expectations. This means that economic means should help to improve social welfare.
1963	McGuire	Social responsibility means that companies not only have economic responsibilities and legal responsibilities, but also mean that they have some responsibility for society beyond these responsibilities.
1966	McGuire	Social responsibility refers to the obligation of a person to consider the impact of his own decisions and actions on society. Merchants should be responsible for the needs and interests of those affected by their business practices.
1971	Johnson	A socially responsible company manager must be able to balance the diversity of interests. He must not only fight for the interests of shareholders, but also employees, suppliers, distributors, local communities and countries.
1973	Eilbert and Parket	The concept of corporate social responsibility consists of two phases. First, it means not doing things that disrupt the neighborhood. Second, it may be expressed as a voluntary responsibility to help the community solve problems. Therefore, perhaps the best way to understand corporate social responsibility is to understand it as "being a good neighbor".
1987	Chengqiu Wang	Corporate social responsibility is the response and solution of the company to social issues.

Time	Author	Definition
1987	Chunhou Xu	The social responsibility of commercial enterprises is the responsibility of maintaining public interest, protecting economic growth and promoting social development objectively existing in the marketing process.
1990	Jiafang Yuan	While striving for their own survival and development, enterprises must face the social needs and various social problems and must fulfill their obligations in order to safeguard the fundamental interests of the country, society and human beings.
1997	Junhai Liu	Corporate social responsibility means that an enterprise cannot simply seek profit for its shareholders as its sole purpose but should have the obligation to safeguard and enhance the interests of other entities in society.
2003	Strategies	Corporate social responsibility often refers to a company's contribution to the sustainable development of society. Sustainable development is defined as the ability to meet the needs of contemporary development without affecting future needs. Therefore, it is generally understood to focus on how to achieve the integration of economic and environmental social rules.
2003	Van Marrewijk	Corporate sustainability and corporate social responsibility refer to the voluntary activities of enterprises, including defining and demonstrating the relationship between the environment and stakeholders in the enterprise operations.
2005	Zucheng Zhou	Corporate social responsibility refers to a comprehensive responsibility that the enterprise should undertake, targeting stakeholders, including economic responsibility, legal responsibility and moral responsibility.
2007	Antal and Sobczak	Corporate social responsibility includes the concepts of culture and socio-economics.
2008	Dahlsrud	Corporate social responsibility includes environmental responsibility, social responsibility, economic responsibility, stakeholder responsibility and resource responsibility.
2008	Matten and Moon	Corporate social responsibility reflects the impact of social rules and corporate business activities on society. It includes clear communication strategies and practices in which companies make contributes to society.
2009	Goldberg	Corporate social responsibility is inseparable from environmental factors.

International scholars have defined the definition and scope of corporate social responsibility to varying degrees. In this research, we will continue to adopt the definition of corporate social responsibility proposed by Chengzu Zhou and add "environmental responsibility" into the content according to the particularity of the research object. Therefore, corporate social responsibility refers to a comprehensive responsibility that the enterprise should undertake, targeting stakeholders, including economic responsibility, legal responsibility, moral responsibility and environmental responsibility. The specific content of corporate social responsibility will be explained in Chapter 4.

2.2 Theoretical Bases

2.2.1 Social Contract Theory

The Social Contract Theory (SCT) was first proposed by Hobbes. He believed that the contract between the superior and subordinate was the origin of national politics. Then, Locke Rousseau and others further perfected the social contract theory with the idea of liberalism. Although their views are different, they all think that social contract is a high abstraction of interpersonal relations, and interpersonal and social relations. In 1937, Coase introduced the theory of social contract into the field of corporate management and defined the enterprise as a combination of contracts in his article T*he Nature of Business*. He considered that companies had upgraded their short-term contractual relationships to stable long-term contracts to reduce transaction costs. Coase's definition of enterprise made the foundation for other researchers to study corporate social responsibility with contract theory. In 1953, Bowen proposed the concept of "publicized enterprise". He believed that corporate activities involved many interests of customers, employees, and society, and depended on these objects. Therefore, enterprises should assume social responsibility. In 1975, Vogel acknowledged that corporate activities significantly affected the external environment of the enterprise. However, the external environment could not restrain corporate behavior, so external environmental stakeholders should make contracts with enterprises, and stipulate mutual rights and obligations.

Thomas Donaldson and Thomas Dunphy think that there is a basic agreement between business and society, that is, the social contract, which reflects the various relationships between business and society. Some are presented in legal form, others in various other forms of contract. This kind of agreement between enterprises and society will change with the changes in economic and social structure and ideology. For example, half a century ago, the only social responsibility of a company was to provide products and services to the society at a reasonable price, thereby maximizing the interests of shareholders, but today companies are responsible for social equity and the life quality of stakeholders. For enterprises, the social contract of enterprises is not as clear as the economic and legal systems they face, and corporate social responsibility is more complicated. In real life, corporate social responsibility should be adjusted according to the changing needs of stakeholders. What social responsibility should be undertaken by enterprises depends on the expectations of stakeholders closely related to the company, depending on the game of power between the company and the society, enterprises and stakeholders, and what kind of consensus is finally reached.

Enterprises often show passiveness in fulfilling their social responsibilities, and the deeper reason lies in the intricate contradictions of the relationship between enterprises and society. To solve this contradiction, it is necessary to realize the unity of all aspects of interests, especially the high unity of corporate interests and society, and explore the combination point of corporate and social development, so that corporate social responsibility is no longer an additional burden for enterprises but turns into the core competitiveness of enterprise development. Management guru Michael Porter pointed out the reasons for the low performance of CSR behavior: first, they treat enterprises and society in opposition and the two are dependent; second, they only talk about public welfare in general, and never combine it with the strategic needs of the company itself. Only by finding a common point with the society can an enterprise truly embark on the path of sustainable development.

After the 1980s, more and more scholars applied social contract theory and research on corporate social responsibility, to obtain a reasonable explanation of corporate social responsibility. In 1982, Donald outlined the tacit relationship between the individual collections of enterprises and their activities. He believed that the theoretical and ethical relationship of the contract formed the binding force of the enterprise, and made the enterprise take the initiative to assume social responsibility. Norman Bowie analyzed the relationship of responsibility between the company and the external environment with economic time as a link.

Based on international research, Chinese scholars analyze CSR from the perspective of contract. Changxi Liu analyzed the boundary issue of CSR with the social contract theory and stakeholder theory (Liu, 2005). Quanlin Guo analyzed the impact mechanism of consumers on CSR from the perspective of contract. In the same year, Shuying Li summed up the Chinese contract theory and proposed that each economic link of the enterprise would produce a certain contract, and the social relationship would have an impact on the contract (Li, 2007). Jianqiu Liu took as the standard to measure the scope and level of CSR (Liu, 2011). Social contract has answered the question of why companies should fulfill their social responsibilities.

2.2.2 Stakeholder Theory

The generation of stakeholder theory dates to the 1960s. Ansoff (1965) was the first economist to officially use the term *stakeholder*. He officially used *interests* in his book *Corporate Strategy*. He believes that to develop an ideal corporate goal, it is necessary to comprehensively balance the conflicting claims of many stakeholders in the enterprise, which may include managers, workers, shareholders, suppliers and customers. In the 1970s, stakeholder theory began to be gradually accepted by Western companies. The economist Dill once described the influence of stakeholder theory as that: We originally thought that the stakeholder's point of view would affect the company's strategic decision as an external cause. But changes have shown that we are moving from Stakeholder influence to Stakeholder participation (Dill, 1975). Subsequently, Wharton School in Pennsylvania opened a stakeholder management course in 1977. It aims at applying the concept of stakeholder to corporate strategic management, and gradually forms a relatively perfect analytical framework. After that, the stakeholder theory first developed widely in Northern Europe. The founder of the Nordic stakeholder thought was Eric Rhenman. In the book *Corporate Management in a Changing World* coauthored with Bengt Stymne, Rhenman illustrates the rise of the stakeholder approach as a theory. They use a theory built on a stakeholder basis to illustrate how a business operates. The conclusion is that a business is a social system in which different stakeholders play distinct roles.

The academic circles considered the Strategic Management: A Stakeholder Approach, published by Freeman in 1984, as a sign of stakeholder theory. According to Freeman, stakeholders are all individuals and groups that can influence the achievement of organizational goals or are affected by the achievement of organizational goals. In Epstein's view, CSR is to make the outcome of corporate decision-making beneficial or not harmful to stakeholders. The result of corporate behavior is the focus of corporate social performance (Epstein, 1987). Therefore, the relationship between enterprises and stakeholders has become the consideration scope of CSR and the most influential focus issue. From the perspective of institutional economics, an enterprise is an organization that contains contractual and cooperative relationships of all stakeholders. It exists for acquiring a greater and more stable craft than individual labor, and in order to achieve this goal, enterprises must rely on the object resources such as capital, land, plant, equipment, social system, environment, and other subject resources such as labor, management, market demand, all of which are necessary. All these resources are derived from society, that is, all stakeholders of the enterprise (Dai, 2007).

The company has a series of clearly identifiable stakeholders, who can score and classify these stakeholders according to specific attributes (such as the legality, power and urgency proposed by Mitchell et al.). Different stakeholders have different requirements for their interests, different degree and diverse ways of realization. The balance of stakeholders depends on the matching between the comprehensive relevancy of stakeholders and benefits exchange requirements (Chen, 2003).

The introduction of stakeholder theory and its combination with corporate social responsibility theory have made important contributions to the research and development of CSR theory and practice.

1. The Stakeholder Theory amends the principles of "Shareholders First".

To some extent, the biggest obstacle to implementing CSR is the principle of shareholders first. Represented by Friedman, the shareholders first theory holders believe that the sole purpose of an enterprise is to maximize profits and maximize profits for shareholders. First, shareholders should have control. Second, managers have a fiduciary responsibility to serve the interests of shareholders alone. Third, the goal of the company should be to maximize the wealth of shareholders.

The stakeholder theory advocates: (1) all stakeholders shave the right to participate in the decision-making of the enterprise; (2) the manager has the fiduciary responsibility to serve the interests of all stakeholders; (3) the goal should be to promote the interests of all stakeholders, not just shareholders. According to the stakeholder theory, an enterprise is a contractual union composed of multiple stakeholders. It believes that the company's contribution is not only from shareholders, but also from employees, suppliers and creditors. Shareholders provide material capital, and other stakeholders provide existing material capital and human capital. Human capital and physical capital should have an equally key role, especially in the era of knowledge economy today. The role of human capital has in some ways even exceeded physical capital. The enterprise is no longer a simple collection of physical capital, but an institutional arrangement for the management of specialized investment, which is essentially a collection of various forms of contract. The risks of the enterprise are not borne by the shareholders, and other relevant stakeholders are also taking risks of the enterprise. Therefore, the owner of the company cannot be limited to shareholders, but all stakeholders are the owners of the company. The rights between stakeholders are independent and equal, and they jointly own the ownership of the business.

While challenging the principle of shareholders first, the stakeholder theory cleared the obstacles for the development of CSR theory to a certain extent. As the proposition of CSR theory has always been to change the narrow mission of that the only mission of enterprises is to increase the interests and enhance the value of shareholders, thinking that enterprises should consider the issue from a higher perspective, that is, consider its relationship with all stakeholders, with society, and assume certain social responsibilities.

2. Clarify the obligations of enterprises to undertake social responsibility and the scope of defining responsibility

According to the definitions of CSR, the beneficiaries of CSR are all people in the society, including corporate investors, employees, customers, creditors and beneficiaries of environmental resources, social security and social welfare etc. By taking the corresponding social responsibilities and aiming at the interests of the society, the company contributes to the sustainable development of human beings to the utmost extent. The content of its responsibility includes legal, economic, moral, and cultural and so on. However, there are still many people who oppose the formulation of CSR. They mainly start from the ambiguity of the objects and contents of CSR and think that enterprises should not bear social responsibility. Some commercial law scholars believe that there is no obligation to CSR, because towards questions like who should bear the social responsibility of an enterprise, and who should be the right holder to fulfill it? There is no satisfactory answer to CSR theory so far. The answer is only expressed in general terms by the consumers, the public, and the society as a whole, but these vague groups are difficult to exist as real rights holders. At the same time, they also think the obligation content of corporate social responsibility also has ambiguity. CSR does not clearly stipulate its obligations to act, nor can it play the role of a code of conduct. If it is reflected in legislation, it may become a blank rule that legislation should have avoided as much as possible.

According to current understanding of stakeholders, it generally includes both the first-level stakeholders that affect the survival of the enterprise, and the secondary stakeholders who do not affect the survival of the enterprise but affect the enterprise or are affected by the enterprise. Although the scope is broadly defined, it clarifies the basic framework of stakeholders as follows: investors, employees, customers, suppliers, creditors, industry associations, local communities, political groups, etc. Unlike CSR research that only generally consider that companies must bear various responsibilities for the entire society. Many international scholars who study CSR and stakeholder theory believe that the concept of stakeholders can be introduced in CSR research. Carroll (1991) believes that stakeholder theory should be applied to the study of CSR. By borrowing it, it can point the direction for CSR, and define the scope of CSR for each major relevant interest group. Clarkson (1995) also said that stakeholder theory can provide a theoretical framework for CSR research, in which CSR is clearly defined in the relationship between business and stakeholders. As Evan and Freeman (1993) said, stakeholder theory cannot replace CSR, but it can be regarded as an important condition for the study of CSR, it can be embodied in the CSR. At this stage, we still need to use stakeholder theory to help us define the scope of CSR. This is both possible and necessary. Enterprises can first clarify the social responsibility of each stakeholder in the framework of stakeholder theory.

3. Provide a way to study the relationship between CSR and its economic performance

Although some people still have doubts or even criticisms about the concept of CSR, the views on CSR have been accepted by more and more scholars and the public (including the business community). Of course, scholars who support this view are also faced with such an arduous task: to seek a more convincing empirical basis, so that more people, especially the business community, will accept the concept of CSR. Let them realize that CSR is not only beneficial to the whole society, but also beneficial to the enterprise itself, so that they can take the initiative to assume corresponding social responsibilities. But the results provided by the relevant empirical research institutes at this stage cannot achieve these. Soon after the theory of CSR was put forward, many scholars only studied the relationship between CSR and economic performance from the fuzzy social responsibility, and the conclusions were naturally inconsistent.

Today, decades after the development of corporate social responsibility research, people's answers to this question are still not uniform. For example, Hillman and Kim (2001) used event research methods to draw conclusions from large sample regression analysis, resulting that they were positively correlated and the two are causal. Geoff Moore (2001) used sixteen metrics to measure CSR. Conclusion was drawn from a study of eight companies in the UK supermarket industry, that there was a negative correlation between social performance and economic performance in the same period. And the previous economic performance is positively correlated with future social performance. At the same time, he also found that the maturity and size of the company were positively related to its social performance. However, he did not find that as the company assumed social responsibility, its current and future economic performance would be improved.

Others have studied the relationship between corporate philanthropy (as a form of CSR) and economic performance. Bruce Seifert et al. (2003) found that whether a company's philanthropy is expressed in cash or in any other form, and whether the company's economic performance is measured by accounting or market methods, the amount of cash resources available to the company is positively related to the donation in cash form, but it has not found that the charity behavior of the company has a clear relationship with its economic performance. Therefore, in this situation, it would be very difficult to convince companies to take the initiative to assume social responsibility.

If the stakeholder theory can be introduced in this research process, the results will be different. Bernadettem Raf (2001) etc. believe that on the study of the relationship between corporate social performance and corporate economic performance, stakeholder theory can provide a framework. They studied the relationship between corporate social performance and the economic performance of firms, using accounting methods in this framework. It turns out that when the management of the company meets the needs of different stakeholders, the economic performance of shareholders will increase. Specifically, the change in corporate social performance is positively correlated with the sales of the company in the current and subsequent years, which indicates that the company's improvement in social performance has short-term benefits, and the sales profit of the third economic cycle of the enterprise and its social performance change. There is also a significant positive correlation between the sales profit of enterprise in the third economic cycle and the change of social performance, which indicates that the improvement of enterprise social performance is beneficial to its long-term economic performance. Such a statement will undoubtedly make many companies willing to take the initiative to undertake social responsibilities and have greatly promoted the good situation in which the whole society finally formed a company to compete for social responsibility.

2.2.3 Management Synergy Theory

According to Dictionary of New Words, synergy refers to the coordination and synchronization between the constituent elements and the system. The purpose is to achieve the overall unity of the system, the stability of the structure, the order of evolution and the maximization of functions. Synergetics is a new discipline that formed and developed based on multidisciplinary research since the 1970s. It was founded by the famous German physicist H. Hake. In 1971, he proposed the concept of synergy in his book *Synergy: a science of cooperation.* By observing many objective systems (such as laser systems), Hake et al. found that there is a general principle in the evolution of systems, that is, subsystems in any system can generate new stable and ordered structure through a purposeful self-organizing process. Hake found that whether it is an equilibrium phase transition or a non-equilibrium phase transition, the reason why the system is disordered before the phase transition is due to the fact that there is no cooperative relationship between the subsystems in the system, and each line is disorderly, so it is impossible to produce an overall nature; and once the system is dragged to the phase transformation point, these subsystems seem to be guided by some kind of "elf", which can quickly change the previous disorder state, then act in a highly organized manner that leads to a sudden change in the macroscopic nature of the system.

With the deepening of system science research, the management community has gradually begun to accept the idea of synergy. Ansoff proposed the concept of synergy in his book *Corporate Strategy*. He believes that the synergy refers to the overall business performance of the enterprise group formed by simple summarization, with respect to each independent component, that is, the relationship of coexistence between enterprises, which is generated based on resource sharing. Hofer and Schendel argue that synergy is the joint effects that result from the aggregation of the individual components, and they emphasize the importance of synergy between synergistic elements. Hiroyuki Itami divides corporate resources into physical assets (production factors, plant, technology or skills, etc.) and invisible assets (trademarks, technical expertise and management skills, etc.). He believes that synergy is achieved by invisible assets. The so-called synergy is hitchhiking, that is, invisible assets developed from a certain part of the company can be used in other fields at the same time and will not be depleted.

According to Robert Buzzell and Breadley Gale, synergy refers to the higher profitability that can be achieved as a company in a portfolio than as a single-operator. The way in which synergy creates value includes the sharing of resources or business behavior, the diffusion effect of marketing and research and development, similarity of enterprise and sharing of enterprise image. Porter studied the relationship between business units through the value chain approach. This association helps people to further understand the synergy, that is, the synergy, popular saying is like "1+1=3", which is the activity of enterprises sharing resources among business units. Chinese scholar Guoping Zeng believes that synergy reflects the state and trend of maintaining cooperation and group among things, systems or elements. On this basis, Jinxiang Chen believes that synergy is characterized by a balanced and orderly structure through joint action of connection, cooperation, coordination, and synchronization, to obtaining the largest target resources, and is based on the premise of less competition and greater efficiency. It is a mode of action resulting from mutual promotion and common development. Youjin Liu and Jiping Yang believe that the synergy is the consistency or harmony of the organic combination, collaboration, cooperation among the internal elements of things or systems in the process of connection and development.

2.3 Research Status

Corporate social responsibility (CSR) has been an important research area in the fields of economics, sociology, management, philosophy, and law since the 20th century. Research is mainly concentrated in the enterprises and home country of enterprises, but at the international level, the research is rarely involved. With the emergence of economic globalization and regional economic integration, especially in the context of "the Belt and Road", there are more and more opportunities for companies along the China-Mongolia Economic Corridor to go abroad or cooperate with foreign companies. The economic and political status of the international community has become more and more important, and its social responsibility has gradually attracted widespread attention from governments, international organizations and theoretical circles, and has become a hot issue of research. At present, research on CSR for cross-regional operations or cooperative enterprises focuses on the following aspects:

1. Motivation of undertaking responsibility

Research by J. Levis (2006) et al. pointed out that transnational corporations adopt CSR guidelines to promote their social responsibility programs, and as measures to adjust their social, environmental and human rights issues. It was mainly due to the pressure of stakeholders. On the one hand, transnational corporations continuously published their social responsibility plans, increased their social responsibility promises. However, the implementation of social responsibility had been weakened, which had attracted public reprimands and even lawsuits. In the US federal courts, here were cases in which transnational companies use corporate codes of conduct as mitigating punishments. On the other hand, in the absence of effective incentive and compensation mechanism for enterprises performing social responsibility, transnational corporations' social responsibility will increase the cost of their operations, and managers lack the motivation to adopt CSR standards. Currently, the motivation for transnational corporations to fulfill their social responsibilities comes from the gradual improvement of social responsibility requirements. In other words, transnational corporations promote their commitment to fulfilling their social responsibilities and publish their code of conduct. The internal reason is the value of transnational corporations and the impact on the maintenance of corporate reputation. The real reason comes from external pressures and influences (such as peers, trading partners, host countries, government NGOs, international groups, etc.). As for how transnational corporations fulfill their social responsibilities, the extent of their implementation depends on the legitimacy, authority and enforceability of the CSR Guidelines.

2. Ecological responsibility

The sustainable development strategy has been widely adopted by the international community, countries and local governments and the business community. Sustainable development considers economic growth, environmental protection, social equity and decision-making in business plans (Schmidheiney, 1992). Many transnational companies have realized that the implementation of sustainable development strategies for the long-term return of enterprises, and the benefits of being a good corporate citizenship for reducing operating costs, improving financial performance, and enhancing corporate brands. They have all announced environmental performance reports. The contents of the report generally include environmental protection plan and principles of sustainable development, how to be an environmental citizen, how to act as an environmental citizen and what's the contribution to sustainable development by doing this, and what are the influencing factors of being an environmental citizen etc. But these reports are not extensive and exhaustive, that can measure the behavior of environmental citizenship quantitatively.

D. A. Rondinelli and M. A. Berry (2000) proposed a model of corporate citizenship and sustainable development, based on a review of relevant literature and analysis of environmental protection reports of 38 transnational companies, such as 3M, ABB and Alcoa. The model is constructed from four aspects: the actions, the plans, the impacts and the outcomes of the environmental citizenship of transnational corporations. The Environmental Citizenship Program of transnational corporations is positioned both internally and externally. Externally positioned actions include employee engagement incentives, philanthropy support, and stakeholder protection; internal positioning includes increased flexibility in environmental policy, prevention of pollution, redesign of products and production processes, energy conservation and resource recycling, and resource conservation. The result of internal and external influences is global sustainable development.

3. Host country responsibility

T. Donaldson (1989) introduced ethical theory into the study of social responsibility of transnational corporations and proposed that the social responsibility of transnational corporations in the host country included improving the welfare of consumers and employees, respecting human rights and social equity, minimizing harm or negative impacts. S.C. Amba-Rao (1993) absorbed and inherited the ethical theoretical basis of T. Donaldson et al., and discussed the relationship between transnational corporations, host countries and subsidiaries supported by the host government, international organizations and other relevant stakeholders from the perspective of business ethics and developed an action and policy agenda through the company and the host government. The interactive relationship of transnational corporation is composed of the "home country government (related interests, society) ⟷ transnational corporation ⟷ international organization (subsidiary) ⟷ host country government". Transnational corporations and countries have internal responsibilities and use their activities to achieve their socio-economic goals. Relevant interest groups assist them in their completion.

In contrast, J.L. Laughlin (1994) and others argued that ethical theory cannot ensure that transnational corporations fulfill their social responsibilities and proposed a model for the development of social responsibility market strategies for transnational corporations. The model consists of a perceptual plane and a behavioral plane. The necessary conditions for the formation of the perceptual plane are common features, including the fair, reasonable and balanced perceptions and international standards of transnational corporations, society and trading partners; a behavioral plane requires reciprocity, consisting of the behavior of transnational corporations, societies, and trading partners. The exchange of social responsibility acts on the behavioral plane through the international standards of the perceptual plane.

On the other hand, some scholars had discussed the causes of conflicts between transnational corporations and host countries and proposed corresponding countermeasures. J. Bennett (2002) argues that the main causes of conflicts are threefold: corruption, poverty and social unequal treatment. Corruption breeds from a lack of integrity, information asymmetry and effective government mechanisms, while poverty and social injustice are rooted in increased global economic risks. As the main body of the world economy, transnational corporations should take different measures to deal with before, during and after the conflict, and do an excellent job in conflict prevention, crisis management and post-conflict strategy reform.

Based on a systematic review of the relevant research literature on politics and transnational corporations, corruption and transnational corporations, CSR and transnational corporations, P. Rodriguez (2006) et al. integrated the three aspects of politics, corruption and CSR, and put forward a research model on the three-dimensional integration of politics, corruption and CSR of transnational corporations. They believe that in the non-market economy, transnational corporations must respond to the host country's rules and regulations and different stakeholders, to adapt to the diversified social and political environment, so that conflicts between transnational corporations and host countries occur from time to time. To ensure the sustainable development of the economic and social environment, transnational corporations must adapt to this non-market economy environment, face the corruption of various governments, officials or individuals and fulfill their corresponding responsibilities to society.

L. Calvano (2007) proposed a framework for analyzing conflicts between transnational corporations and local societies (host countries) from the perspective of relevant stakeholders in the host country. The framework argues that the reason for the increase in conflict between transnational corporations and host countries stems from the difference in stakeholder power inequality, stakeholder perception gap, and cultural context. The inequality of capabilities hinders the development of the relationship between transnational corporations and host countries in a win-win developing model. If this non-reciprocal relationship exists, the relationship between the host country and the transnational company will be subject to the will of the transnational company. At the same time, transnational companies will spend time and money to resolve these conflicts. Therefore, the solution to the conflict between transnational corporations and host countries is to increase the host country's understanding of transnational corporations, and to cultivate the ability of host countries to compete with transnational corporations.

Chinese enterprises have been concerned about CSR for a brief time. The awareness of CSR is not deeply rooted in corporate culture. In the vast number of developing countries with more investment in Chinese enterprises, due to the low economic level, the attention and requirements of these host governments and people for CSR are not slim. This makes the threshold of social responsibility in China low. Enterprises pay more attention to short-term economic benefits, fail to integrate political, social and environmental information and responsibilities into their business decisions, and fail to elevate corporate social responsibility to the strategic level. However, with the development of the CSR movement on a global scale, the host country's awareness of social responsibility is getting stronger and stronger, and transnational enterprises will inevitably cause some contradictions and conflicts in the local area. Many overseas investment companies in China are in mining, construction and other industries. Some enterprises are affected by the negative factors, such as short-term profit drive, lack of environmental awareness, weak awareness of safety in production and insufficient technical level, which objectively cause many accidents and problems in the investment behavior of the host country (Shen and Zhang, 2016).

Yuan Chufeng (2017) put forward from the legal point of view that Chinese foreign investment enterprises must undertake corporate social responsibility from the international law and domestic law to conduct joint supervision and collaborative governance. Huang Lingyun et al. (2018) used the game method to compare the social responsibility of transnational corporations and host countries, under the conditions of complete rationality and fairness and reciprocity. The results show that in the case of fair reciprocity, transnational corporations should bear more social responsibility, and the host country can achieve win-win cooperation by sacrificing some of the benefits to improve the investment environment or tax incentives. Some scholars have also studied the social responsibility of mining enterprises in foreign investment. They believe that the social responsibility of mining enterprises for foreign investment has not only the problems related to the social responsibility of general transnational enterprises, but also their uniqueness, which needs to be treated seriously (Wang, 2014).

Throughout the existing achievements of social responsibility research on transnational operations and investment enterprises, the following characteristics or deficiencies are presented: First, the research field is scattered, and a unified and generally accepted research system has not been formed. Second, the total amount of research is small, and most of them are still at the initial stage of "what is", the research on "why" and "how to do" has hardly progressed. Third, most of the current literature mainly focuses on the social responsibility of transnational corporations in developed countries. However, the issue of social responsibility for developing countries' transnational corporations operating in developed countries or other developing countries has not received enough attention. Fourth, most of the theoretical researches were to examine CSR issues from the perspective of government and society, and lack of consideration for the coordination and interaction between enterprises, home countries and host countries. To this end, this research intends to explore the issue of social responsibility fulfillment of resource-oriented enterprises in the China-Mongolia Economic Corridor from a collaborative perspective, and how China and Mongolia can jointly promote the implementation of resource-oriented CSR.

Chapter 3

CSR Implementation Status of Transnational Resource-oriented Enterprises

3.1 Overview of Resource-oriented Enterprises in CMEC

Mongolia is one of regions with the most abundant natural resources in Northeast Asia. In the medium and long term, there is enormous potential for development. In recent years, China and Mongolia have had more economic exchanges, and China's investment in Mongolia has also increased rapidly year by year. Chinese enterprises are investing in mineral resources development, construction engineering, processing of animal products and food production in Mongolia. Most of the direct investment of Chinese companies is concentrated in the field of mineral energy. This is mainly because: First, in recent years, to meet the needs of China's rapid economic and industrialization process, the demand for resources is very strong, and the output and storage of many domestic resources cannot meet the needs of national economic development, so foreign direct investment in the energy sector is increasing year by year. Second, in 2003, China further determined that the cooperative development of mineral resources and other aspects is one of the key areas for cooperation between China and Mongolia. This has provided broad prospects for the development of bilateral economic and trade relations. Third, China has the advantages of labor, geography, and technology in its resource development cooperation with Mongolia. It can compete with other countries and has created a solid cooperation foundation for China to create cooperation opportunities in Mongolia's resource development.

By the end of 2015, Mongolia's proven reserves of mineral resources have risen to the 7th place in the world, and the space for improvement is still very large. Mongolia is becoming a valuable resource supplier and plays an important role in China's energy diversification and "Belt and Road" layout.

In 2015, China-Mongolia trade accounted for 62% of Mongolia's total foreign trade. Among them, exports accounted for 83.5, 90% of mineral products were exported to China. From 1990 to 2015, China's direct investment in Mongolia was $43.3, accounting for 25.9% of the total stock. China's geopolitical and market demand determines the status quo of Mongolia's foreign trade and direct investment. By the end of 2014, Mongolia had discovered 1,470 deposits and more than 8,240 mining sites for more than 80 minerals. Mainly copper, iron, coal, manganese, chromium, tungsten, molybdenum, aluminum, zinc, mercury, antimony, tin, gold, gold, phosphate, fluorite, asbestos, graphite, mica, crystal, emerald, amethyst, turquoise, petroleum, shale mines, etc. Among them, important mineral resources with great development potential are copper, molybdenum, zinc, coal, iron, gold, tungsten, fluorite, petroleum, uranium, silver, rare earth, shale etc. According to the December 2015 statistical bulletin and related information of the Mongolian Mineral Resources Bureau, as of the end of 2015, the copper mine metal reserves were 45.8 million tons, ranking first in Asia. The three major copper mines currently discovered, respectively Erdente porphyry copper molybdenum ore, chachan suburiga porphyry copper molybdenum ore, and oyu tolgoi porphyry copper gold ore, have been included in the national strategic minerals.

Mongolia's coal reserves are 25.8 billion tons, ranking the top ten in the world. Among them, the striking reserves of the Taben Tolgoi coal mine (TT mine) are calculated to be 6.5 billion tons according to the JORC standard (Australian Mineral Resources and Ore Reserves Reporting Specification), of which about 2 billion tons are coking coal, and the rest are high quality thermal coal. In addition, the Baqal brown coal mine, the Nalin Suhaiite coal mine, and the Xibobao brown coal mine have been included in the National Strategic Minerals List. The metal reserves of the Mongolian iron ore mine are 390 million tons, and the Tumultai iron ore mine has been included in the Mongolian Strategic Minerals List. The metal reserves of Mongolian gold mines are 598,000 kilograms, ranking the top 10 in the world. The Qiuerte gold mine is included in the National Strategic Minerals List. The metal reserves of Mongolian molybdenum ore are 660,000 tons. Mongolia's zinc ore metal is 1.11 million tons, and the Tumultin slag-zinc mine has been included in the Mongolian Strategic Minerals List. Mongolia's fluorite metal reserves are 15.78 million tons, and its output and export volume rank third and second in the world. Mongolia has 125,000 tons of uranium metal reserves, ranking in the top 10 in the world. The Marl uranium mine and the Gulvan Prague uranium mine are included in the National Strategic Minerals List. Mongolia's rare earth ore metal reserves of 1.83 million tons, ranking the world's forefront.

In addition, the proven reserves of phosphate rock in Mongolia are 6 billion tons, ranking first in Asia and fifth in the world, mainly distributed in the lake basin in northern Mongolia. Mongolian oil has proven reserves of 2.438 billion barrels. It is rich in resources and has a large population. It has a land area of 1,566,500 square kilometers and a population of about 300 million. Due to the abundant domestic resources and limited domestic consumption, more exports and the usefulness of the trade economy and the development of resources will be the top priority of China-Mongolia economic and trade cooperation, and it is also one of the core contents of the construction of China-Mongolia-Russia Economic Corridor. In June 2016, the third meeting of the heads of state of China, Russia and Mongolia signed *the Outline for the Construction of China-Russia Economic Corridor*, which indicates that a new window for resource cooperation between the two countries has been opened. China will be the largest source of investment for Mongolia and trading partner.

3.1.1 Metal Mineral Cooperation

1. A model of Sino-Mongolian mining cooperation - Tumultin Oolong Zinc Mine Project

Mongolia Metal Import and Export Co., Ltd. and China Nonferrous Metals NFC Co., Ltd. jointly implemented the Tumultin Oolong Zinc Mine Project. The Chinese side owns 51% of the Xindu joint venture, and Mongolia holds 49% of the shares.

2. Sino-Mongolian Oyu Tolgoi Copper Mine

In early 2007, Mongolia established a working group on the joint development of the Oyu Tolgoi copper mine, marking the official launch of the Mongolian government's strategic goal of rapidly improving the country's overall economic strength through joint development of mineral resources. Mongolian Business Economic Counselor Naren in China said in an interview, in August 2014, that the Oyu Tolgoi Project (OT project) currently being developed in Mongolia is the largest gold and copper project in Mongolia. In the future, it hopes to attract Chinese investment and develop huge mineral resources underground. The Oyu Tolgoi Mining Project is mainly exported to China. It is expected that China's demand for copper will increase significantly in the next 10 years. At present, all the finished products of the copper mine are exported to China, and the electricity used is also provided by China (Han, 2017).

3. Erdente Copper Mine Power Plant Construction Cooperation

The Mongolian Erdente Copper Mine Power Plant Expansion Project was officially started in May 2016. The owner of the project is Erdente Mining Group and the contractor is China Harbin Electric International Engineering Co., Ltd. The expansion contract amounted to US$41.83 million. The expansion project includes four 12MW steam turbine generator sets made in China. After the project is completed, it will inject new vitality into the development of Mongolian mining industry. The expansion of the Erdente Copper Mine Power Plant will become a model for the "the Belt and Road" initiative to be implemented in Mongolia, and a model for Chinese equipment to go out abroad and will also become a new bridge for energy cooperation between China and Mongolia.

3.1.2 Non-metallic Minerals Cooperation

The cooperation between China and Mongolia in the oil industry is increasing rapidly year by year. China is a big country with world-class mining technology and equipment advantages, and a big energy consumer. Mongolia is driving its own economic development with local energy exploitation. It needs to extract a lot of oil to develop the domestic economy. Mongolia's oil exploitation is subject to technology constraints, oil exploration is not much, and it needs China's technical support. So, China and Mongolia have great advantages in oil cooperation. In 2013, China and Mongolia pointed out in *the Long-term Outline of the Strategic Partnership between the People's Republic of China and Mongolia* that the mutual assistance of the two sides in the oil sector should be deepened and reluctant and strengthen the cooperation of the Tamutchao Oilfield and the Zongbayin Oilfield Project. Mongolia has provided many favorable conditions for the development of related projects. The Chinese side strongly promotes domestic enterprises to help Mongolia build a domestic refinery, based on mutual benefit and win-win progress. At the same time, according to the fundamental principle of marketization, China supports the commercial activities of refined oil products between China and Mongolia. The Chinese side will actively explore the possibility of strengthening the supply of refined oil products to Mongolia in accordance with the actual needs of Mongolia. In 2005, Shengli Oilfield invested more than 10 million US dollars to develop the Zongbayin oilfield in Mongolia.

After China Daqing Oilfield Co., Ltd. acquired the development rights in the Tamutaga oil mine in the Eastern Province of Mongolia in 2005, it established a subsidiary in Mongolia and began to formally explore oil. PetroChina Daqing Tamutagag Co., Ltd., in accordance with the products signed with the Mongolian government, will work on the exploration and development of petroleum. Since 2005, PetroChina has operated the Mongolian Tamuzagar project in the role of operator, to carry out oil and gas exploration and development in Mongolia. This project has been one of the most expensive projects invested by China in Mongolia. Its significance is to effectively strengthen the active mutual assistance between China and Mongolia in the energy sector, and to promote the good growth of the Mongolian oil industry. At present, there are 16 companies in the oil industry in Mongolia, and 6 companies are mutually supportive with China. In Mongolia's oil industry, the most important partner should belong to China, and China has injected a lot of capital and vitality into Mongolia's energy and economic development.

3.1.3 China-Mongolian Cooperation with Other Energy Companies

1. China and Mongolia coal resources mutual assistance development

With the rapid development of China's economy, the demand for energy has also increased. Mongolia's coal reserves, however, are abundant. China-Mongolia coal resources cooperation has enormous potential under the complementary advantages of China and Mongolia. The form of cooperation between the two parties in the field of coal is mainly coal trade. Small and medium-sized enterprises have entered Mongolia and invested in coal development. For example, on June 26, 2007, the *Agreement on Mongolia-China Cooperation in the Development of Zhun-Prague Coalfield in the Eastern Province of Mongolia* was officially signed. Jilin Zhongji Group and Mongolia Tarayijiri Mining Company finally signed a cooperation agreement, whereby Jilin enterprises obtained the mining rights of the Mongol Zinn Prague coalfield. According to the signed agreement, 6 million tons of mining capacity will be formed by 2010. Shenhua Group is China's largest coal development enterprise and the first large-scale Chinese enterprise to enter Mongolia. In 2014, Shenhua Group signed a cross-border railway construction agreement with Mongolia. China and Mongolia cooperate to build a cross-border railway. The starting point of the route is China's Ganqi Maodu, and finally arrives at the Gashun Suhaitu of Mongolia. The Gashun Suhaitu of Mongolia is the largest unexplored Tarben Tolgoi coal mine in the world.

Moreover, in addition to the mutual assistance in the construction of this railway, China and Mongolia have also formed a large-scale coal joint venture industry consisting of three companies: China Shenhua Energy Company, Mongolian Eldesta Ben Tolgoi Energy Resources Co., Ltd. and Tarben Tolgoi. In December 2016, officials from the Ministry of Mines and Heavy Industry of Mongolia met with the delegation of China Shenhua Energy Company. China Shenhua proposes to start the power plant, railway construction and mining projects in Taben Tolgoi. Mongolia holds 51% of the shares and Shenhua holds 49% of the shares, to form a company to build a railway from the Tawang Tolgoi mining area to the Sushun Suhaitu port. The term of the investment and cooperation agreement is 22 years, consistent with the operating license term. Mongolian companies hold 51% of the operating rights. The target markets are China and third countries. Subcontractors must be Mongolian companies with a contract period of not less than 5 years.

2. China-Mongolia Gas Cooperation

Due to the small amount of natural gas reserves in Mongolia, China and Mongolia have not made progress in natural gas cooperation. But in the field of energy cooperation, the development of natural gas is indispensable. Inner Mongolia Duowei Energy Co., Ltd. is a subsidiary of China Morita Group. Recently, the company has completed the exploration and development of various natural gas energy sources in Mongolia and has also got the Mongolian natural gas exploitation license. This natural gas mining permit was first awarded in the history of Mongolia, marking the leap-forward progress of Chinese companies in the exploration and development of natural gas in Mongolia. This indicates that the company will own the natural gas exploration rights of 6.656 square kilometers of Mongolian Alatan oil, with an approved reserve of 60 billion cubic meters, and has a natural gas exploration license of about 2 trillion cubic meters. It is in South Gobi province of Mongolia. For the large-scale exploitation of natural gas resources in the two blocks, it is expected that the amount of natural gas delivered to China in the future will be very large. At that time, the shortage problem of clean natural energy resources will be effectively alleviated, and the dependence on natural gas imports will be greatly increased. China's energy security will be greatly improved, and the greenhouse gas emissions will be significantly reduced. The cities with severe haze weather in northern China will also have significant relief, making huge contribution on the protection of ecosystems.

In the energy consumption structure, due to capital and technology constraints, the natural gas or gas usage is virtually zero in Mongolia. The southern and northwestern power supply needs to rely on many imports. In October 2013, the Mongolian Prime Minister signed a coal-to-gas project agreement with Sinopec on his visit to China, investing about 30 billion US dollars, using 50-80 million tons of coal per year to produce 150 billion cubic meters of gas. The project was launched in November 2015 when the President of Mongolia visited China. China has applied advanced technology to Mongolia to further promote the development of energy cooperation between China and Mongolia. Mongolia's desire to export high value-added products also requires China to provide advanced technology. Mongolia hopes to enhance its modern management experience and technology from foreign investment.

Table 3.1 Sino-Mongolian cooperative resource-oriented enterprises

Classification	Project	Chinese Enterprise	Cooperation direction
Metal mineral cooperation	Oyu Tolgoi Copper Mine		The first batch of copper was exported to China in July 2013. Most of the minerals produced by this mine copper mine are shipped to China.

Classification	Project	Chinese Enterprise	Cooperation direction
	Erdente Copper Mine	Harbin Electric International Engineering Co., Ltd.	In May 2016, the expansion project of the Mongolian Erdengte Copper Mine, which was built by China Harbin Electric International Engineering Co., Ltd., officially started.
Non-metallic minerals cooperation	Songbayin Oilfield	Shengli Oilfield	In 2005, Shengli Oilfield invested more than 10 million US dollars to develop Mongolian Zongbayin oil.
	Tamuzag Oil Mine	PetroChina Daqing Tamutagag Co., Ltd.	The total investment amount is 100 million US dollars. In 2013, the production of crude oil in the Tamutzag oil field exceeded 800,000 tons.
	Zhuen Prague Coalfield	Jilin Zhongji Group	The coalfield has a storage area of 25 square kilometers, and is high-quality long-smoke lignite with an average burial depth of only 5 to 10 meters. The initial proven reserves are 730 million tons, equivalent to more than 73% of the entire Jilin Province's coal reserves.
	Taben Tolgoi Coal Mine	China Shenhua Group	China Shenhua proposes to start the power plant, railway construction and mining projects in Taben Tolgoi. The route starts in Ganqi Maodu, China, and ends in the Gashu Suhaitu of Mongolia, which has the largest unexploited Tamu Tolgoi coal mine in the world.

Classification	Project	Chinese Enterprise	Cooperation direction
Other energy	Alatan Oil and Gas	Inner Mongolia Duowei Energy Co., Ltd. under the Morita Group of China	The Inner Mongolia Duowei Energy License for Natural Gas Exploitation Energy was first awarded in the history of Mongolia. The Alatan oil and gas area is 6566 km square kilometers of mining rights, natural gas reserves are 60 billion cubic meters, and Mongolia South Gobi Province, It covers an area of about 40,000 square kilometers and is estimated to have a reserve of about 2 trillion cubic meters of natural gas, based on exploration data from the former Soviet Union.
	Coal gas project	Sinopec	It has invested about 300 billion US dollars, 50-80 million tons of coal per year, and produced 15 billion cubic meters of gas.

3. Other clean energy cooperation.

Mongolia's solar and wind energy resources are abundant. The Chinese side is actively researching the *Asian Super Grid Plan* proposed by the Mongolian side. The plan will introduce Chinese capital, technology and talents, and the output of electricity will be exported to other countries such as China and South Korea. China and Mongolia have a large amount of cooperation in power. The special geographical location makes Mongolia's solar and wind energy more abundant than other countries. Based on satisfying their own needs, it can also build a high-voltage power grid to transport electricity to other countries. On March 16, 2017, at the invitation of the Mongolian Ministry of Energy, the chairman of China Datang Corporation went to Ulaanbaatar, Mongolia for a working visit. Mongolia hopes that China Datang will play an advanced power generation and environmental protection technology and carry out cooperation and discussion on Ulaanbaatar power and heat planning and hotspot joint production projects to achieve win-win cooperation. In November 2015, the Mongolian President visited China. The Mongolian Ministry of Energy and China State Grid Corporation signed *the Agreement on the Feasibility Study of the China State Grid Corporation and the Mongolian Ministry of Energy on the Cooperation of the Xiboao Coal-fired Power Transmission Integration Project*. Agreement pointed out that the main body of implementation is China's State Grid Group, which mainly carries out related work on coal mines and power plants in the Xiboao project. In the case of Mongolia's national strategy for green development, it is indicated that renewable energy such as wind and solar energy should be vigorously developed. Relying renewable energy to 20%-25% is the target before 2020.

Under the background of the China-Mongolia Economic Corridor, China-Mongolia economic cooperation is increasing, and the cooperation of resource-oriented enterprises will become closer and closer. Mongolia's abundant domestic resources and low resource development technologies have made Mongolia's resource development always maintain a high appreciation space. Therefore, the economic and strategic deployment of the "the Belt and Road" strategy will be exerted by the strength of the China-Mongolia Economic Corridor. More enterprises go abroad to supplement the lack of domestic resources and strive to make win-win progress of mutual benefit.

3.2 CSR Definitions of Transnational Resource-oriented Enterprises in CMEC

Scholars have defined the content of CSR from different angles and divided it into a series of specific actions or tasks that the company is responsible for the society, which makes the social responsibility of the enterprise concrete, and helps to put forward specific implementation measures. Among them, the more representative ones are the "Corporate Social Responsibility Pyramid" proposed by Carroll (1979), the "Triple Bottom Line" proposed by John Ellington (1997), and the Two-level Theory proposed by Stephen Robbins (1997). Based on the particularity of the research object, the content of social responsibility of resource-oriented enterprises in China and Mongolia is defined as economic responsibility, legal responsibility, environmental protection responsibility, moral responsibility and charity responsibility.

3.2.1 Economic Responsibility

The economic responsibility of China-Mongolia resource-oriented enterprises mainly includes the following two aspects:

First is to form a mutually beneficial economic form. Mongolia's mineral resources and other natural resources are abundant, and the strategic mineral reserves are among the highest in the world. It can be said that Mongolia is the only pillar industry that conforms to the characteristics of modern industry. Mongolia has always been the four major industries of resources, agriculture and animal husbandry, automobile maintenance, processing and wholesale and retail. In terms of the proportion of GDP (Gross Domestic Product) in Mongolia, the resource industry has been hovering between 19-20% in recent years and has always been in the position of the largest industry. It has increased since 2012. In 2015, it reached a peak of 24.97% (see Figure 3.1). Resource enterprises themselves are capital-intensive industries, and Mongolia's resources are basically mining and primary processing industries. Therefore, the main driving factor is obviously the capital investment.

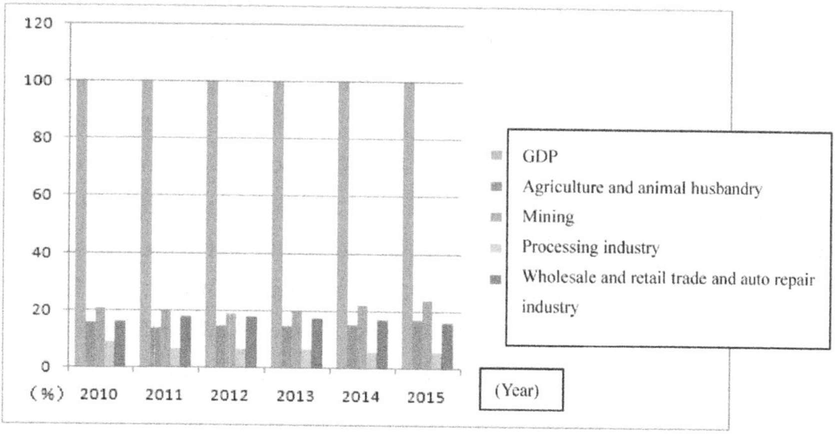

Figure 3.1 GDP shares of the four major industries in Mongolia
(Source: Mongolian Bureau of Statistics website, http://www.1212.mn)

According to Figure 3.2, starting from the financial crisis in 2009, the total investment in the strong foreign capital inflows climbed and continued until 2012. After that, the total investment fell sharply under the rapid contraction of foreign capital. In 2015, it was about doubled compared with 2012. At the same time, in these years, except for 2014 and 2015, foreign capital is higher than domestic capital, and the foreign capital spurt inflows are even more than double that of domestic investment in 2011-2012. The foreign capital injection of the industry is 2.5% of the foreign direct investment stock of 17.563 billion US dollars between 1990 and 2015. This also shows that Mongolian mining and other resources are the main industries that attract foreign investment. From the data analysis given, the foreign capital flow is highly consistent with Mongolia's GDP growth trend, and the peak year of foreign capital flow is also the peak period of Mongolia's GDP growth.

Therefore, the development of Mongolian resource-oriented enterprises is one of the important strategies for Mongolia's economic development. Especially in recent years, Mongolian mineral resources play a significant role in the economic development of Mongolia. However, due to the relatively low consumption of the national market in Mongolia and the backwardness of technology, the development of most resources such as minerals relies heavily on foreign investment. As Mongolia's largest trading partner, China has established extensive cooperative relations with Mongolia in terms of resource development and infrastructure construction. It reflects the complementary advantages of the two countries in terms of economics and provides necessary conditions for strengthening bilateral relations. In the strategic deployment of the economic corridors between China and Mongolia, a mutually beneficial situation has been formed. For China, the problem of lack of resources has been solved. And for Mongolia, it is one of the important responsibilities of resource-oriented enterprises to obtain more foreign investment, improve the country's GDP, and get rid of economic poverty.

The development of Mongolian mining industry is deeply affected by the foreign capital flow, which are caused by the fluctuation cycle of the international bulk cargo market and the domestic policy and regulatory environment. The adjustment of mineral regulations and the decline of international bulk cargo prices have caused the collapse of foreign capital flows, which not only directly affected the sustainable development of the mining industry, but also indirectly affected the coordinated development of related industries, and in turn aggravated the expansion of Mongolia's fiscal deficit and debt increase. There are many problems and challenges in the development of Mongolian mining industry, but the favorable factors are also obvious, that is, the non-renewability and scarcity of natural resources, the rich mineral resources and the promising prospects etc. The overall mining-oriented strategy cannot be changed in the long run. China has maintained its position as the world's No. 1 demanding country for a long time. The demand from Japan and South Korea is huge. China and other countries are implementing energy diversification strategies with strong investment incentives. The construction of the China-Mongolia-Russia Economic Corridor will greatly improve the infrastructure and financing environment of Mongolia.

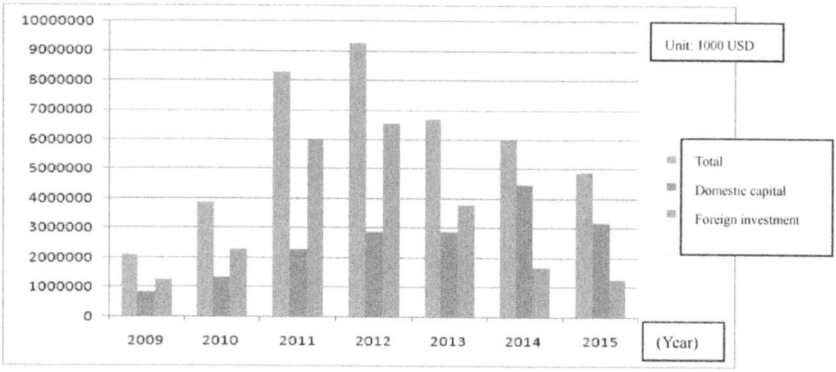

Figure 3.2 Domestic and foreign investment structure trends in Mongolia (Source: Mongolian Bureau of Statistics website, http://www.1212.mn)

Second is to enhance industrial competitiveness and promote the leap-forward development of China and Mongolia. The imbalance of regional economic development is a widespread problem in all countries of the world. This imbalance is manifested in many aspects, such as education, human quality, economic development level and natural environment. However, the imbalance between regions is mainly reflected in the economy. Therefore, realizing the leap-forward development of the regional economy is the basis for realizing the overall improvement of the whole region. As the world's second largest economy, China jointly develop with neighboring countries and support pillar industries. The energy industry shoulders the heavy responsibility of promoting the economic development of the Asian region. Therefore, it is an unshirkable responsibility of resource-oriented enterprises to rationally plan the industry, improve the competitiveness of the industry through technology and information, and realize the leap-forward development of Mongolia and China.

3.2.2 Legal Liability

Paying taxes according to law is the legal obligation of enterprises, and resource-oriented enterprises are certainly no exception. Enterprises are the creators of social wealth, and the government is the manager of social wealth. The government relies on the legal operation of enterprises to pay taxes, centrally manage the overall wealth of the society, and implements the fair distribution of social wealth through price, taxation and welfare policies. Enterprises can reasonably and legally avoid taxation, but they must not evade taxes. The former is the legitimate rights and interests of enterprises, while the latter is the illegal behavior of enterprises that do not bear social responsibility. Mongolia's legal environment is unstable, with low level of legal supervision and enforcement. For resource-oriented enterprises, good contact with residents and protection of their legitimate interests are crucial. Due to the insufficiency of Mongolia's relevant resource laws and some other factors, the superposition of numerous factors led to the Resource Nationalism Trend in the whole country of Mongolia in the early 21st century (Hugjiltu, 2017). It became the direct incentive for the Mongolian parliament and the government to over-express and even exclude policies and regulations. This has caused the relationship between resource-oriented enterprises and residents to fall to the freezing point, which has seriously affected the normal operation of resource-oriented enterprises. Therefore, rational management of the relationship between the two countries, in accordance with the law and avoid unnecessary conflicts, is the statutory social responsibility that resource-oriented enterprises should perform.

3.2.3 Environmental Responsibility

The development of resource-oriented enterprises not only determines the development of the national economy, but also brings environmental problems that cannot be ignored, such as surface subsidence, three wastes (waste water, waste gas, and waste residue), noise and many other environmental damages, and environmental pollution problems. The three wastes generated during the exploitation, processing and production of resources are: mineral water with high salinity, suspended solids, acid and alkali, and special pollutants. It is important to solve the problems of surface subsidence, waste and noise caused by the production and processing of resource enterprises. Seriously solving the problem of surface subsidence, three wastes and noise caused by the production and processing of resource enterprises is a major event to improve the sustainable and stable development of resource enterprises.

Resource-oriented enterprises have direct impacts on the environment such as dust, noise, etc., as well as indirect effects such as traffic and traffic accidents that increase due to changes. How to deal with and solve the environmental problems of resource enterprises and create a better production and living environment for employees is a major event related to the safe production of energy resources and the development of energy economy. It is one of the keys to the sustainable development of resource-oriented enterprises, as well as the social responsibility of long-term cooperation between the two countries and the sustainable development of the natural environment of the earth.

Mongolia is a landlocked country, and its ecological environment is very fragile. One third of the Mongolian soil is the Gobi Desert, most of which are grasslands and mountain grasslands, and the ecological environment is very fragile. Disasters such as droughts, sandstorms, dragon whirlwinds, and water shortages often affect Mongolian residents. The natural resource itself is an industry of great environmental risk. Firstly, the mining industry needs to drain the groundwater to break the balance of surface water and groundwater, which will easily lead to the exhaustion of rivers and lakes. Over the years, a large number of dry rivers and springs in Mongolia have been unreasonably exploited, especially in relation to the mining of gold deposits. Secondly, the south, which is rich in mineral resources, is the Gobi Desert area. The water resources are scarce, the surface water is difficult to meet the needs of humans and animals, and the mining industry can only use deep ground. According to estimates by

Mongolian experts, the use of shallow and deep water in the mining area is currently 1:9, which has seriously broken the local water cycle balance. Experts put forward the proposal of Transferring the Northern Water to South, but the problem is that it is difficult for Mongolia to rely on its own strength to achieve this costly project. Third, wastewater discharged during mining and processing often poisons humans and animals. Finally, the transportation of mineral products mainly by road caused severe damage to grassland and highway facilities.

The development process of Mongolia's mining industry is also a process of increasing environmental awareness among the Mongolia people. The positive role of the Resource Nationalism Trend is to urge the government to introduce laws that are environmentally friendly, responsible, transparent, and in line with international standards, which are conducive to the implementation of a sustainable vision. Mongolia is a country close to the north of China. The natural environment of Mongolia directly affects that of China. If Mongolia is dry all year round, it will cause spring dust storms and little rain, which will directly affect the northern part of China's climate. For example, spring dust storms and droughts will occur in the Inner Mongolia, China.

Therefore, solving the environmental problems of resource-oriented enterprises is directly related to the environmental problems of the two countries. Environmental issues are one of the responsibilities that resource enterprises cannot ignore in the context of the China-Mongolia Economic Corridor.

3.2.4 Moral Responsibility

The moral responsibility of resource-oriented enterprises in the China-Mongolia Economic Corridor can be divided into the following aspects:

1. Save energy

Economic activities and activities to transform nature must not exceed two limits: the resources taken from nature should not exceed the regenerative capacity of nature; the waste discharged into the natural environment should not exceed the self-purification capacity of the environment. Most of the natural resources are non-renewable resources, the proliferation ability is very poor, and limited resources must be effectively utilized. The prerequisite for the development of the resource-oriented industry itself is that there are sufficient resources. Mongolia's resources can be economically exploited in the top ten in the world, and there is huge room for appreciation. But natural resources are mostly non-renewable resources and therefore very valuable. Unreasonable or indiscriminate exploitation is a huge waste, which has a significant impact on the local natural environment and the country. It will also have a negative impact on China's sustainable development in the long run, and it is likely to cause various disputes between resource companies in the two countries.

As Mongolian citizens have a keen sense of environmental protection, it is not conducive to the development of Chinese enterprises in the local area. Therefore, it is possible to cause unnecessary conflicts. Resource-oriented enterprises save energy, rationally and efficiently exploit resources, is a problem that cannot be ignored in the operation of resource-oriented enterprises and is also a due responsibility. Therefore, it is the greatest social responsibility of resource-oriented enterprises to save resources, increase the recovery rate, and improve the utilization efficiency of coal resources in the production process, as well as the inevitable choice of their own survival and development.

Since China's resource exploitation technology is still not very advanced, many enterprises lack a sense of conservation. Therefore, the previous mining process has caused a lot of resources to be wasted. Now, it must be advocated that coal enterprises should have the awareness of resource conservation, the production technology needs to be improved, the waste should be reduced, and the mining period of resource enterprises should be extended, to benefit future generations.

2. Work safely

Most resource companies have high-risk industries. Mongolia's unique production environment and specific production technologies, such as backward resource development technology, lack of professional technicians, and underdeveloped transportation, require resource- oriented enterprises to put safety work in a particularly prominent position. In Mongolia, production safety includes personal safety and livestock safety in the production process. Mongolians are more nomadic. Therefore, attention should be paid to the safety of personnel and animal husbandry in local mining and transportation.

The safe development of enterprises is the concrete embodiment of the important thinking of "Three Represents" and the scientific development concept in the security field of resource-oriented enterprises. It reflects the essential requirements of the scientific development concept. Correctly understand the relationship between safety and development, safety and production, safety and efficiency, put safety production work at the strategic level of enterprise development, synchronize planning, simultaneous deployment, and simultaneous advancement, ensure safety in production, and truly implement the policy of "safety first, prevention-oriented, and comprehensive management", so as to create a safe and efficient mine, realize the healthy and sustainable development of the coal industry, and fulfill the humanitarian social responsibility of caring for people's livelihood.

3. Protect employee rights and improve labor relations

Labor relation is a special relationship between people. It is expressed as a collection of power and rights, cooperation and conflict. Essentially, it reflects the social and economic interests between people. The population of 3 million people in Mongolia is mostly in Ulaanbaatar, the capital of Mongolia. There are fewer residents and less labor. In resource-oriented enterprises in Mongolia, people can even see field workers from foreign countries. Some resource companies have relatively poor production conditions and complex staff structure. They need to implement the people-oriented business philosophy, undertake the main social responsibility of achieving harmonious development of labor relation.

Responsibilities of the company include abiding by the laws, regulations and policies concerning labor security in Mongolia and China; undertaking the obligation to maintain the coordination of labor relations; overcoming the discriminatory ideas and behaviors in the process of hiring employees; signing legal and effective labor contracts; promoting a scientific and democratic human resource management system; participating in accordance with the law and pay various social security fees on time and in full; paying the labor remuneration on time and in full; providing safe and healthy working conditions and environment; caring for employees' life difficulties and physical and mental health; creating a harmonious corporate culture; improving the quality and level of employees.

3.2.5 Charity Responsibility

Erdene experts in the Mongolian University of Finance and Economics mentioned that Mongolian nationals have a poverty level of 29%, and some regions are 40%-43% poor. There are many difficult groups in the society, many children in poor families drop out of school because they can't afford tuition; many elderly people who are lonely are helpless; many people with disabilities are embarrassed because they have no ability to work; when natural disasters come, the victims are homeless and so on. There is no stable source of income, etc. Currently, it requires enterprises to take some responsibilities for the country, take the initiative to bear the charity responsibility, pay more attention to the public welfare undertakings, and help these people to tide over the difficulties. This not only reflects the ability of the enterprise, but also reflects the sense of social responsibility of the enterprise. The public will have a good impression on companies that actively undertake charitable responsibilities, which will enable the company to have a mass base, and contribute to the long-term development of the company (Zhang, 2011).

Responsibility of enterprises for public welfare undertakings can be expressed as helping people living in poverty, donating money and materials to solve their food and clothing problems; subsidizing social welfare institutions and charities to provide life assistance for the elderly, the weak, the lonely, and the disabled; when natural disasters occur in the region, they actively raise funds and materials to help the people in the disaster areas overcome the disaster; integrate the public welfare into the culture of the enterprise, and enable the employees to actively and actively help the people around them. Mongolian experts pointed out that the more local resource-oriented enterprises, the higher the local poverty rate. Places such as South Gobi and Moral League are places with more natural resources and more enterprises, but unfortunately these places have even higher poverty rate. Therefore, relevant experts in Mongolia pointed out that the implementation of social responsibility of resource-oriented enterprises is not enough, and the fulfillment of charitable responsibility is not high. Most companies only pursue corporate profits and ignore the livelihoods of residents.

Many school-age children in these pastoral areas are unable to attend school on time due to poverty and insufficient investment in pastoral school construction. Many families have unstable incomes and cannot provide tuition fees. Moreover, resource-oriented enterprises have a cyclical nature. After the mining work or resource development in a certain region, no plan is implemented to consider the long-term livelihood of residents. As a result, with the withdrawal of resource-oriented enterprises, the herders lost their jobs one after another. Areas that have been mined are no longer suitable for the development of animal husbandry, which makes more herders unable to be self-reliant. Some enterprises need professionals to mine resources and work, so they cannot provide employment opportunities for residents. However, due to the high impact of natural resources exploitation on the local environment, the herdsmen are even more difficult to maintain a livelihood, and lead to higher levels of poverty. Based on these circumstances, the company must assume social responsibility, conduct public welfare undertakings within the local capacity, and make efforts to solve the problem of school-age children and the livelihood and employment of residents.

3.3 CSR Implementation Status of Transnational Resource-oriented Enterprises in CMEC

3.3.1 The Contribution of Transnational Resource-oriented Enterprises in CMEC

1. Contributions in international relations

China and Mongolia have a long-standing trading partnership. Since 1998, China became the largest investor of Mongolia, and now China is Mongolia's largest trading partner. China and Mongolia have always maintained friendly partnerships. The partnership has enabled the rapid development of China and Mongolia's economy, which has contributed to a win-win model of mutual benefit. Mongolia's economic development in recent years has attracted the world's attention. Mongolia has a unique resource reserve. With the current increasing demand for resources, Mongolia has become the focus of international attention. Countries are increasingly demanding investment in Mongolia, and the trade of coal resources in Mongolia plays a key role. The coal currently exported by Mongolia is a rare natural mineral, which has played a huge role in the economic development of Mongolia. To attract more investors, the Mongolian government has formulated a strategy of attracting investment, developing the mining industry and revitalizing the economy, which also provides favorable conditions for the cooperation between China and Mongolia to develop Mongolian resource-oriented enterprises (Han, 2017).

The effective cooperation between China and Mongolia in this field will be beneficial to the economic revitalization of Mongolia, social development and the expansion of economic cooperation between China and Mongolia. This is of practical significance for China to implement the development of the western region, and to develop the economy, by leveraging the traditional advantages and geographical advantages of economic cooperation between China's Northern provinces and Mongolia. It is of great strategic significance to establish a long-term partnership of good-neighborliness, friendship and mutual trust between China and Mongolia in the 21st century. In the long run, to maintain

China-Mongolia economic and trade cooperation, and maintain new development, it is necessary to open up a field of cooperation, and the cooperation between China and Mongolia to develop Mongolian resources is an effective way to fundamentally expand bilateral economic and trade relations (Ma, 2007).

In 2014, Chinese president Xi Jinping visited Mongolia. After the two sides met through high-level leaders, the bilateral economic ties between China and Mongolia began to tighten. The China-Mongolia-Russia Economic Corridor proposed in 2016 is one of China's key cross-regional economic corridors. This is also the strategic basis of China's "Belt and Road" strategy. The relationship between the two countries has developed rapidly, and the economic environment of the two countries has been continuously improved. These positive factors have prompted the two countries to conduct trade cooperation. China-Mongolia trade, especially coal and other mineral trade, plays a pivotal role in Mongolia's foreign trade share. It is a good trend for China to increase trade with Mongolia under the conditions of advanced technology and rich experience. The trade cooperation will inevitably have a good impact on the two countries. At the same time, China has the advantages of geography and labor in the mineral development cooperation with Mongolia, which also creates opportunities for China's mining industry in Mongolia and lays a solid foundation for cooperation. Good economic and trade cooperation can provide dedicated support for the China-Mongolia-Russia Economic Corridor and the "the Belt and Road" strategy. Therefore, the development of Mongolian resource enterprises is of great significance to both Mongolia and China.

2. Economic contributions

Mongolia is a country with vast land, large resource savings, and certain development potential. It is rich in mineral resources such as coal, gold deposits, tungsten tin, copper concentrate, gold, iron, zinc, etc. According to the latest statistics, Mongolia's total coal reserves are about 175 billion tons (including inferred reserves) (Xie, 2017). It is one of the world's largest coal exporting countries. These resource-oriented enterprises have led the rapid development of Mongolia's economy, and promoted the upgrading of the industry.

Resource exports account for a substantial proportion of Mongolia's trade with many countries, only exports of mining companies can reach nearly 80% of trade exports. The development of resource-oriented enterprises plays a significant role in Mongolia's economic growth. In 2010, Mongolia's main mineral resources (coal, copper concentrate, iron ore, crude oil, zinc concentrate, unsorted semi-finished gold) exported 1.27 tons, with a year-on-year growth of 127%, including 15 million tons of coal exported to China. In 2011, the export volume of Mongolia's main mineral resources (coal, copper concentrate, iron ore, crude oil, zinc concentrate, unsorted semi-finished gold) was 168 million tons, with a year-on-year growth of 32%, of which 21 million tons of coal were exported to China. In 2012, the export volume of Mongolia's main mineral resources (coal, copper concentrate, iron ore, crude oil, zinc concentrate, unsorted semi-finished gold) was 189 million tons, with a year-on-year growth of 12.5%, of which 7.08 million tons of coal, 2.587 million tons of concentrated copper, 12,000 tons of gold, 1.577 million tons of iron, and 151,000 tons of zinc were exported to China. Since 2010, the export volume of Mongolia's main mineral resources (coal, copper concentrate, iron ore, crude oil, zinc concentrate, unsorted semi-finished gold) has increased, as shown in the following table:

Table 3.2 Exports of Major Mineral Resources in Mongolia (RMB 10,000)

Mineral Resources	2010	2011	2012	2013	2014	2015	2016
Coal	9096.66	11384.04	12269.24	10248.79	11645.58	8965.2	13812.53
Copper concentrate	371.09	368.58	370.62	393.29	797.56	90.53	1061.74
Iron ore	189.198	3438.07	4074.93	4049.54	3596.82	3031.15	3583.66
Zinc concentrate	1349.43	1482.14	2127.31	3023.83	4322.12	5097.71	5376.73
Crude oil	77.02	83.84	81.8	90.59	62.65	66.05	81.85
Unsorted semi-finished gold	3.42	1.82	1.49	4.67	5.19	6.63	9.48

(Source: www.1212.com)

The promotion effect of Mongolia's resource exports on its economy is shown obvious. Resource export has been an important source of national income, accounting for 32% of government revenue and 30% of Mongolia's gross national product. Among them, China-Mongolia trade, especially coal and other mineral trade, has occupied a prominent position in the share of Mongolia's foreign trade. Among the many resource-oriented enterprises in Mongolia, MAK and Mongolian mining companies have achieved fruitful results. Among them, China's Shenhua, Chinalco and other large central enterprises are active in this field. These companies are constantly developing, cooperating and innovating. Most of the successful coal source cooperation so far has been private enterprises. Among them, China's private enterprise Qinghua Company and Mongolia MAK have obtained licenses to jointly develop part of the resources of Nalin Suhai Coal. The current production capacity of this mine is maintained at 3 million tons per year (Xie, 2017).

The impact of China-Mongolia cooperation resource-oriented enterprises on the local economic development of resource development is also significant. For example, the mining industry will increase local fiscal capacity through wages, savings, local procurement, business development, expenses and other financial flows, and the development of the mining industry can gain value. Mining products and mining companies' capital and services can promote local economic development through catering services, electricity supply, and transportation services. On the other hand, suppliers in the region sell their raw materials to the mining industry, and the benefits will increase economic activity, so that through joint creation, the final exploitation of resources will help reduce poverty.

As China's economy continues to grow, the demand for energy is increasing. China is a big energy consumer. In the past three years, its energy consumption has reached more than 400,000 tons per year, ranking first in global energy consumption, and China is striving to increase energy consumption year by year to maintain stable economic development, as shown below:

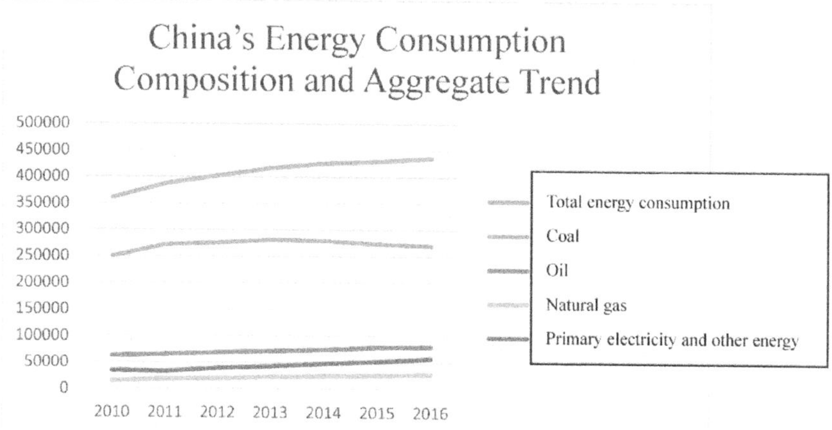

Figure 3.3 China's Energy Consumption Composition and Aggregate Trend

(Source: China Statistical Yearbook 2016)

Figure 3.3 China's Energy Consumption Composition and Aggregate Trend

(Source: China Statistical Yearbook 2016)

In 2010, China's total energy consumption was 360.648 million tons. In 2011, China's total energy consumption was 387.43 million tons, a year-on-year increase of 7%. In 2012, China's total energy consumption was 402.138 million tons, a year-on-year increase of 4%. In 2013, China's total energy consumption was 416.913 million tons, a year-on-year increase of 4%. In 2014, China's total energy consumption was 425.806 million tons, a year-on-year increase of 2%. In 2015, China's total energy consumption was 429.905 million tons, a year-on-year increase of 1%. In 2016, China's total energy consumption was 4.36 billion tons, an increase of 1% year-on-year. Due to China's policy reasons, coal consumption has decreased, but the total energy consumption is still growing. It is still very difficult for China to adjust the energy structure in the short term. It needs to be improved slowly. So, coal will remain the dominant fuel in China's energy composition in the future.

The growth rate of coal consumption is expected to reach a peak soon, which will push the proportion of coal in the total primary energy demand to increase by 3,070 around 2020, reaching a peak of 66%. Then, this rate will begin to fall back, and will fall to 63,070 by 2030. In the future, the power industry remains the main area of coal consumption, accounting for more than two-thirds of the increase in demand. As heavy industry will grow rapidly soon, coal demand in the industrial sector will also grow rapidly.

For the source of energy, China needs to import energy while producing its own energy. Australia, Indonesia, Mongolia, Russia, and Vietnam are all energy importing countries of China. The high-quality coking coal and some thermal coal produced by Mongolia will still be one of the important energy imports of China. Therefore, the Sino-Mongolian coal trade cooperation is the most important core of economic and trade cooperation between the two countries. Good economic and trade cooperation can provide dedicated support for the China-Mongolia-Russia Economic Corridor and the "Belt and Road" strategy, and make the Chinese economy continue to develop.

3. Contributions in social livelihood

Resource exploitation will inevitably affect the people's livelihood, and it will help local governments, local enterprises, cooperatives, and youth etc. Resource development develops and utilizes the labor resources of residents in the form of local management and civic participation. Residents provide capacity building to resource-oriented enterprises. Local administration supports these policies for the employment development of local communities. Resource-oriented enterprises can increase the opportunities for local people, especially young people, to find employment. Mongolia has special regulations. When foreign-funded enterprises in Mongolia employ employees, the number of employees in Mongolia is not less than 51% of the total number of employees. This has helped young people improve their employment rate and improve their work skills. This has helped young people improve their employment rate and improve their work skills, but also increased women's Employment opportunities for other ethnic minorities and vulnerable groups. Local governments can also increase the sources of funding, health and social infrastructure for local vocational education through investment in resource-oriented enterprises and help increase local development capacity.

For example, Sino-Mongolian joint venture Xindu Company, established in 1998, is one of the successful industry models in China-Mongolia cooperation trade. The company has accelerated the development of Mongolia's economy in compliance with the law, tax payment and continuous operation. Under the theory of sustainable development, it also assumed its own responsibility to the local people's livelihood and increased the employment rate of local residents. At present, the company has 215 workers in Mongolia, which has led to an increase in Mongolia's GDP of 2.5, which has accelerated Mongolia's economic development. The company also actively participated in the local public welfare work, which was supported by the local people and quickly developed the local economy. At the same time, it also played an incentive role for other local coal mining enterprises. Sino-Mongolian joint venture Xindu Company also aids the local education and health system. For example, it will fund 20 college students in Sukhbaatar province each year and provide an X-ray room for local general hospitals (Ma, 2007).

Many resource-oriented enterprises also provide certain vocational training programs. Such training programs obviously increase the knowledge base and ability of local residences. When signing local contracts according to the laws of resource-oriented enterprises, it may include hiring local vocational education professionals. Vocational education is also bound to become a job opportunity in the region. There are also opportunities to contribute to other development projects (technical staff work in infrastructure projects), which has also reduced the number of outsiders, and has had a positive impact on local social relations.

Resource development projects have the potential to enhance the infrastructure of local communities. Infrastructure is essential for the development of remote areas, while at the same time increasing the advantages of developing modern technologies and new skills for local enterprises. For example, Sino-Mongolian joint venture Xindu Company invested 110 million and set up a 15-kilometer optical cable line in West Uralt County, which connects the mobile phone network commonly used in Mongolia, enabling local residents to have information channels to communicate with the outside world. Investment in resource development projects will also include local construction, agriculture, road investment, etc. For example, Sino-Mongolian joint venture Xindu Company has built a Unity Park for West Uralt and repaired the road of West Ural.

Some resource-oriented enterprises conduct researches on topics such as human resources, marketing, finance, and manufacturing technology. To this end, they work with government agencies and professional organizations. Some companies list a list of locally available goods and services and provide them with the necessary requirements and support. It aims at increasing opportunities for local companies to become suppliers to mining companies, and supporting local development, by promoting effective planning and organizational development in the market. For instance, some herders and agricultural cooperatives supply meat and dairy products to the mines.

3.3.2 Problems in CSR Implementation of Transnational Resource-oriented Enterprises in CMEC

Mongolia has attracted many foreign-funded enterprises by its rich resources, supplying the raw materials of various countries and bringing great benefits to its own country. However, the exploitation of resources is always a double-edged knife. It can not only bring benefits, but also bring negative influences. Under the great temptation of interests, enterprises do not assume responsibility for the social environment, occupy land, chase indiscriminate development, and ruin the environment. The residents, who are victims, can only maintain their lives in a hostile environment without the corporate responsibility.

Due to the geographical location and ecosystem, Mongolia is one of the climate sensitive countries. The climate is caused by the development of Mongolia from history to the present. The exploitation of the resources on the atmosphere has led to various problems, such as climate change disorders in Mongolia. Climatic conditions, however, play a very important role for farmers and herdsmen. Mongolia is in a dry area. The water supply is the main basis for livestock migration. It is very important for the quality of sustainable livelihoods of local farmers and herdsmen. When the mining expands, and the water consumption increases, it will not only affect the total water consumption, but also affects water quality. Due to the exploitation of resources, many environmental problems have arisen. For example, there are several stages in the mining project from exploration to its closure. The environmental impacts of each mining stage are different, so the ecological and environmental problems caused by mining enterprises in the process of mining are listed according to relevant information, as shown in the following table:

Table 3.3 Environmental Issues Arising from the Mining Process

Mining Process	**Influencing Factors**	**Major Environmental Problems**
Exploration (mine exploration)	Surface vegetation, water quality, soil, noise, livestock	Chemical spills destroy surface vegetation, pollute water resources, disrupt normal livestock activities, and destroy forests, cause air pollution and noise pollution.
Mining	Soil, surface vegetation, wildlife, air quality, water quality, noise and vibration	Destroy forests, occupy natural habitats, destroy soils, sediments in rivers, reduce well water levels, reduce streams, disrupt normal activities of wild animals, increase dust, deteriorate water quality, chemical spills destroy surface vegetation, cause air pollution, land desertification, geological collapse, and noise pollution.
Production	Soil, surface vegetation, wildlife, air quality, water quality, noise and vibration	Destroy the soil, cause sediments in the river, pollute water resources to reduce water availability, cause air pollution, destroy forests, occupy natural habitats, increase dust; Increased acidity in mine water (metallurgy and coal mines); Underground and surface water cyanide contamination (metallurgy); Chemical leakage causes damage to vegetation, soil erosion, land desertification, geological collapse.
Closure (production reduction and closure)	Soil, surface vegetation, water quality, wildlife, air quality	Tailings piled up, groundwater level dropped, ore tailings collapsed, destroyed surface vegetation, polluted water resources, land desertification, geological collapse, affected normal activities of wild animals; Increased acidity in mine water (metallurgy and coal mines); Underground and surface water cyanide contamination (metallurgy).

The environmental impact of mining activities cannot be ignored. What's more, resource development also poses a series of problems for the farmers and herdsmen in the development area. According to the level of the problem, and the degree of influence of farmers and herdsmen, these issues are divided into ecological environment issues, economic issues and social issues. As shown in Table 3.4:

Table 3.4 Problems brought about by the Resources Exploitation for Farmers and Herders

<table>
<tr><th>Problem Category 1</th><th>Specific Description</th><th>Problem Category 2</th><th>Impact on the Survival and Development of Farmers and Herdsmen</th></tr>
<tr><td>Ecological environment issues</td><td>Destroy surface vegetation, cause soil erosion, land desertification, geological collapse, air pollution, and noise pollution.</td><td rowspan="2">Direct problem</td><td>Mainly affect and destroy the living environment</td></tr>
<tr><td rowspan="2">Economic issues</td><td>Land acquisition and land occupation.</td><td rowspan="3">Mainly affect and destroy the production environment</td></tr>
<tr><td>Production water consumption is reduced, grazing grassland area is reduced, affect the traditional life of farmers and herdsmen, and the income of farmers and herdsmen is reduced, ecological compensation costs are low and difficult to implement, and the proportion of compensation is unreasonable.</td><td rowspan="2">Indirect problem</td></tr>
<tr><td>Social issues</td><td>Unemployment and re-employment difficulties, difficulty adapting to new environments, returning to poverty.</td></tr>
</table>

1. Ecological environment issues

The Taben Tolgoi Coal Mine is a large open pit mine in the South Gobi province. It was the world largest unexplored mine in 2014. At that time, the survey found that the coal seams were intact, and in this year, China Shenhua Company launched the mining, power plant and railway construction projects in Taben Tolgoi. The Mengfang coal mine detection expert detected that the bottom of the mine is a single-dip formation, gently inclined from north to south. The coal seam is great thick, with clear horizontal layers and two sets of mutually perpendicular joints. The top gap is filled with a thin layer of sulfide, and the lower crack is filled with a grayish white calcium film. The coal briquettes are brittle and light, contain a small amount of mud, low gray dust, and are high quality coking coal.

The Taben Tolgoi coal field is a lake-type sedimentary coal field, controlled by the paleo-geomorphology of the basement, with small dip angle, simple structure, thick coal seam, good quality, shallow burial, and is suitable for large-scale open-pit mining (Sa, 2015). The mining of this coal has brought great economic benefits to China and Mongolia. Since the mining of the area from 2014, it has contributed a lot to the economic and social development of the two countries. At the same time, however, the ecological environment has been seriously damaged. Due to the coal mining in the Taben Tolgoi coal mine, the air quality has been seriously degraded, the frequency of dusty weather has increased, the surface vegetation has been destroyed, the water resources have been polluted, the land has begun to be decertified, and even the normal life of the local residents has been disturbed. Exploring its causes goes back to the coal companies that exploit coal resources in Taben Tolgoi.

Mongolia has arid climate, high altitude and low precipitation (260 mm in the Altai region and 60-260 mm in the Gobi region), so it is most of groundwater, and a small part of the surface water that does not evaporate. In Mongolia, more than 90% of water comes from groundwater, and more than 55% of it is used for mining and industrial purposes. According to the Asian Development Bank, by 2010, Mongolia's water consumption will reach 321 million cubic meters per year, excluding water and electricity consumption, and the root cause of the impact on Mongolia's water quality is the production and operation activities of resource-oriented enterprises. At present, water resources management is the most important and complicated problem for resource-oriented enterprises. According to incomplete statistics, so far, on average, for every 10,000 tons of coal mined, 0.2 hectares of grassland will be collapsed, and an average of 2 tons of sewage will be discharged for every ton of raw coal mined. According to the survey, the mining will lead to a large amount of drainage, and the groundwater level in the mining area will drop, which naturally affects the water balance of the mining area and disturbs the equilibrium system of surface water and groundwater.

In July 2013, the South Gobi Citizens Representative Conference, which had implemented several large-scale mining projects, had issued a decree prohibiting groundwater from being put into use in 2016. However, the decree is about to be revoked, the public is protesting the country's strong policies, and the public is calling for coordinated management of groundwater resources. To eliminate the negative impact of mining on the past, countries, international organizations and communities need to hold companies accountable for water pollution, increase productivity and manage them properly. In addition to the chemical spills of these resource-oriented enterprises, the surface vegetation and the surrounding animal habitats are directly or indirectly affected. It also exacerbates soil erosion, geological collapse, etc. What's more, the large-scale accumulation of waste generated during the mining process (such as tailings, coal-sparing stones, etc.) has caused excessive occupation of grassland, and disrupted the life of wild animals, destroyed normal ecosystems.

In addition to surface pollution and water pollution, pollution caused by resource production also includes noise pollution and air pollution. The machinery and equipment used in the production of resources are all large-scale machinery and equipment, which will make a loud noise during the operation of the machine and bring noise pollution during the transportation of resources. Noise pollution will inevitably affect the lives of residents. It will also affect the living habitat of natural living things. Polluted gases emitted during resource extraction, such as carbon dioxide, carbon monoxide, and a large amount of dust, will inevitably cause serious pollution to the atmosphere, which is not only harmful to residents, but also affects other cities in the vicinity and other countries.

Mongolia is a country close to the north of China. The natural environment of Mongolia directly affects that of China. If Mongolia is dry all year round, it will cause spring dust storms and little rain, which will directly affect the northern part of China. For example, spring dust storms and droughts will occur in Inner Mongolia. Therefore, solving the environmental problems of resource-oriented enterprises is directly related to the environmental problems of the two countries. Therefore, environmental issues are one of the responsibilities that resource enterprises cannot ignore in the context of the Sino-Mongolian Economic Corridor.

The environmental expenses of China-Mongolia resource-oriented enterprises are the costs of preventing environmental problems and avoiding major pollution problems. In order to effectively develop resources and reduce the surrounding environmental pollution caused by resource development, enterprises need to increase their investment in human, material and financial resources, namely, the environmental protection costs and prevention costs. In addition, in the development and production process, resource-oriented enterprises need to regularly conduct knowledge training on ecological environment for staff, teach environmental protection law, related legal responsibilities and social responsibilities, which are education costs. At the same time, enterprises need to monitor the surrounding environment of resource development on a regular basis, that is, monitor costs. And R&D and development costs to reduce costs and control environmental pollution etc. are preventive environmental costs for resource-oriented enterprises to prevent environmental problems and avoid pollution. In the case that resource-oriented enterprises have fulfilled their CSR, the environmental pollution problem is relatively small, but for many enterprises, driven by the interests, it is difficult to ensure that the local environment is not polluted.

2. Economic issues

Herders in various regions of Mongolia have always used traditional animal husbandry as their main mode of production. However, the problems of land occupation and pollution caused by resource development not only make momentous changes to the living environment of herders, but also have a great impact on the traditional life and production methods of herders. Of course, it has caused a certain economic burden on herders.

As resource-oriented enterprises occupy the land, the grassland area of herders is reduced, and the grassland is degraded, resulting in a decline in the total income of herder families. With the accelerated development of mining projects, larger playgrounds are occupied by some resource-oriented enterprises, the grassland areas used by herders for grazing are getting smaller and smaller, and the herdsmen's livestock are gradually decreasing. These situations have caused big economic pressure on them. The coal mining, power generation, chemical projects, etc. carried out on the open pit mine of Taben Tolgoi Coal Mine have caused the degradation of nearby grasslands and the desertification of the land. The open pit coal mines continue to expand, which has a significant impact on the income of herders. The development of the Taben Tolgoi coal-fired power base also affected the lifeline of the downstream grassland, forests, wetlands and other ecosystems, resulting in the desertification of grassland, the loss of water resources and even the source of sandstorms, which also seriously affected the agriculture and animal husbandry. With the large-scale expansion of coal-fired power bases on the grasslands, large-scale industrial development such as coal mining, coal-fired power generation, and coal chemical industry has become one of the main causes of grassland desertification. In addition to the dilemma of reducing the area of grassland, it also faces the problem of rising dairy mortality caused by waste and dust emissions from nearby coal mines.

For resource-oriented enterprises, the enterprise operations not only consume a large amount of natural and labor resources, but also may have a great adverse impact on the surrounding environment and residents. As mentioned above, the resources production will inevitably cause air pollution. Emissions will also affect water resources quality. In particular, the occupation of grassland will increase the economic pressure of residents and may even lead to a return to the poverty, resulting in more serious local economic problems. It is the responsibility of the enterprise to restore the destructive ecological environment, and to solve the problem of local herders. The corresponding costs will also occur in the enterprise.

Environmental recovery and governance costs are the costs of the company to recover and manage the damaged or polluted minerals and ecological environment. It generally includes the cost of water resources and air purification, the cost of treatment for landslides and surface subsidence, and the disposal costs of waste (waste rock, wastewater, etc.). In addition to environmental costs, companies are also responsible for providing appropriate subsidies to residents. At present, the ecological compensation fees for local farmers and herdsmen in China-Mongolia cooperative resource-oriented enterprises are low and difficult to implement. When resource-oriented enterprises enter the grassland to mine coal, regardless of their intensity and breadth, their damage to the grassland is far greater than that of animal husbandry. However, the compensation and payment of construction land for the mining area is far from being able to compensate for all aspects of damage caused by resource development. The compensation for the land acquisition of farmers and herdsmen in the mining area is also low, and the distribution ratio is unreasonable.

3. Social issues

Mining has brought many tough challenges to many resource-rich countries, including corruption, conflict, poverty, social vulnerability and environmental impact. According to the 2011 International Corruption Impact Indicators Index, only one-fifth of the top 25 countries rely on oil and mineral exports. About 500 million people around the world live in the most resource-rich countries, and their lives are not rich. Eco-environmental problems and economic problems are the direct problems caused by resource enterprises when they exploit resources. Social problems are deeper problems caused by ecological problems and economic problems.

Grassland pastoral areas are scarce in water resources, but a large amount of water resources are needed in the process of resource exploitation, which will affect the quality of life of grassland local herders, thus worsening the contradiction between grassland herders and resource-oriented enterprises. Moreover, the large-scale occupation of grassland by resource-oriented enterprises undermines the survival mode of traditional animal husbandry development. It reduces the income of herders who live on livestock, and even causes some people to lose their jobs, limiting herders' right to subsistence and development, which has affected the development of the local economy. Therefore, leaving traditional animal husbandry and grassland, herders will fall into poverty, and some herders will even lose their basic viability, which will eventually become a serious social problem. For example, resource-oriented enterprises continue to increase mining efforts, resulting in the occupation of land. When this land is closed, there will be many rifts. The surface will collapse, making the lives and survival of farmers and herdsmen face serious difficulties.

In recent years, resource-oriented enterprises have fastened their steps of developing resources. With the acceleration of development speed, the local economy has also achieved unprecedented development, and the lives of residents have gradually improved. However, enterprises always put their interests ahead of responsibility and interests. Driven by the fact that enterprises are increasingly unconstrained in the development of resources, they have not fulfilled their responsibilities to residents, leading to sharp problems between the herders and resource-oriented enterprises. The most important thing is the implied social issues, these more complex and far-reaching social contradictions are emerging. Enterprises exploit the underground resources of the residents indiscriminately, causing unprecedented pollution to other underground resources, such as water resources, and causing great damage to surface plants and soil.

The lack of these abundant resources has seriously affected the residents' lives. Enterprises occupy many living places for farmers and herdsmen, but they have not taken up their due responsibilities. They have not given sufficient compensation, which has destroyed the traditional animal husbandry industry chain of the herdsmen, and damaged the reputation of the company. Farmers and herdsmen are restricted by enterprises to survive and develop, which has greatly damaged their economic interests, thus bringing many ecological and environmental problems, economic problems and social problems.

Farmers and herdsmen have been restricted from survival and development by enterprises. It has greatly damaged their economic interests. And it has brought about many ecological and environmental problems, economic problems and social problems. Although farmers and herdsmen are resistant to the occupation of pastures and the destruction of pastures, they have no ability to fight against it, and can only passively accept it. Therefore, with the further development of the pasture, their survival is further squeezed. The implicit contradiction between farmers and herders and mining companies will continue to deepen and erupt, which will lead to deep social contradictions.

On the other hand, the fulfillment of charitable responsibility of resource-oriented enterprises is not high. More companies only pursue corporate profits, without considering the livelihoods of residents. Many families have unstable economic incomes, and many school-age children are unable to attend school on time due to poverty and insufficient investment in pastoral school construction. Moreover, resource-oriented enterprises have a cyclical nature, but the implementation plans are not considered when the mining work or resources in a certain area are developed, without considering the long-term livelihood of residents. Because of the withdrawal of resource-oriented enterprises, the herdsmen are unemployed, and the mined areas are no longer suitable for animal husbandry development, making more herders unable to be self-reliant. What's more, some companies need professionals when they are working on mining resources, so they cannot provide employment opportunities for residents. However, due to the high impact of the exploitation of natural resources on the local environment, it is difficult for herders to maintain their livelihoods, resulting in higher poverty.

3.4 Causes Analysis of the CSR Implementation Dilemmain China-Mongolian Transnational Resource-oriented Enterprise

1. Chinese companies don't know enough about Mongolia's local culture and laws

Chinese resource-oriented enterprises invest in Mongolia's energy sector, often because of blind competition or catching up with the investment boom, they have not judged the investment environment risk enough, and have not deep enough research on local policies, laws, cultures, etc., and have not recognized their own strength level. They lack experience in foreign investment project operations and business management processes, more importantly, lack of responsibility and international cooperation capabilities, seriously affecting the interests of enterprises, while damaging the image of Chinese enterprises in Mongolia (Jie, 2015).

At present, many Chinese companies have started transnational operations and opened up foreign markets. However, they have encountered many problems in their actual operations. Due to the lack of in-depth understanding of local laws and culture, as well as the lack of certain experience, the conflict with local communities frequently occurred. For example, Chinese companies have labor relations in Latin American countries, and there are trade union organizations that maintain labor relations. However, many Chinese companies in Latin America lack experience in negotiating with trade unions and rely on local governments. The results of local governments to resolve labor disputes are not always ideal. As a result, Chinese enterprises engaged in cross-border business have encountered a lot of trouble in fulfilling their social responsibilities. Most companies are clear about the importance of corporate social responsibility, but it still has some difficulty in fulfilling it.

The people of Mongolia advocate nature and have a strong sense of environmental protection. They have the idea of Resource Nationalism (Hugjiltu, 2017). Mongolia's natural resources are the property of the people of most countries and represent the government's license to the company. According to Article 6.16 of the 1992 Mongolian Constitution, Mongolia's land, forests, water, animals, plants and other natural resources are completely protected by the people and the state. Under this provision, the rights, obligations and benefits of using natural resources will have a stronger impact on groups involved in the mining sector. The Mongolian resource-oriented enterprises in Mongolia did not study Mongolia's laws on natural resources, nor did they have a detailed understanding of the local culture, exploiting local resources at the expense of the Mongolian environment, lacking environmental awareness, and failing to establish corporate social responsibility. It has caused the deterioration of the ecological environment in Mongolia and the waste of energy resources. Such behavior by Chinese companies has attracted strong dissatisfaction from the Mongolian people and has greatly damaged the image of Chinese companies. Residents have great resistance to resource-oriented enterprises and exclusivity to foreign companies. In this context, Chinese resource-oriented enterprises should be cautious in the development and development process in Mongolia, to avoid unnecessary conflicts and accidents.

Mongolia's resource-oriented enterprises have many social responsibility laws, such as the Mineral Law, Petroleum Law, Investment Law, and Labor Law etc. However, China's enterprises in Mongolia have little knowledge of Mongolia's relevant laws. In the process of exploration and mining, there have been great obstacles, and the smooth progress of energy resources cooperation between China and Mongolia has also caused certain problems. On the other hand, some enterprises, regardless of the relevant laws, disregard the interests of local people. Even in the case of the incomplete laws of Mongolia, some enterprises have rubbed elbows with the laws and damaged the interests of the local people in disguised form, and at the same time, they declared that their social responsibility is in place.

Because of the above, the people of Mongolia have always had a bad impression on Chinese companies. International organizations have been investigating in Mongolia for many years. The results show that the country most trusted by the Mongolian people is Russia, followed by the United States, Japan, South Korea, Germany and others. China generally ranks fifth or sixth (Yao, 2010). These realistic factors all indicate that the Mongolian people lack trust in the Chinese people and there is vigilance. This is also an unfavorable factor in the energy cooperation between China and Mongolia. These factors have become the limiting factors for Chinese investment companies in fulfilling their CSR. It is hoped that Chinese resource-oriented enterprises will understand the importance of CSR in the process of resource exploitation. The fulfillment of CSR is not only related to the success or failure of corporate transnational operations, but also to the image of national enterprises, to the mutual benefit and friendly partnership of the two countries, and whether China's "the Belt and Road" strategy can be successfully implemented. The active implementation of social responsibility by enterprises is the maintenance of corporate reputation and investment in brands and is to maintain the country's reputation. In such a fierce competitive environment, enterprises must actively fulfill their CSR if they want to grow and develop.

2. Chinese enterprises' sense of social responsibility has not changed

The awareness of social responsibility of Chinese enterprises is generally low. In the process of rapid development, many companies only look at corporate profits, pursue profit maximization and neglect the fulfillment of social responsibility. Moreover, Chinese enterprises' attention to CSR and its expectations are not high, resulting in a general lack of awareness of CSR in China. On the one hand, compared to other transnational companies, Chinese companies lack experience in implementing social responsibility in the process of transnational operations. For example, the West has many years of experience in fulfilling corporate social responsibility practices. They have a good reputation and a long-term competitive advantage. Chinese enterprises' CSR awareness, however, is not that much strong. The corresponding internal supervision and management mechanism is not perfect, and the monitoring effect on CSR is not good. The governance of CSR practices is still in its infancy. In particular, there are many loopholes in the supervision activities of Chinese transnational corporations' social responsibility practices. On the other hand, Chinese transnational corporations often follow their domestic business experience, and still regard government-enterprise relations as the focus of public relations, while not paying attention to local communities and non-governmental organizations (NGOs) (Jie, 2015).

Without the accumulation of sufficient experience, Chinese transnational companies cannot have the same strong social responsibility fulfillment consciousness and strategy as other Western companies. At present, each country proposes more and more specific social responsibility fulfillment conditions for foreign resource-oriented enterprises. The conditions require not only foreign companies, but also both parties must conduct environmental management and responsibility management from a social perspective. The next trading activity can only be carried out with the consent of the article. More and more phenomena show that in international trade, CSR has become an inevitable trade condition, affecting the relationship between enterprises and their future development. In a socialized environment with developed information, if a company evades fulfilling social responsibilities, or has a negative attitude toward fulfilling social responsibilities, it will lead to the destruction of corporate reputation, and in serious cases, it may cause failed business.

According to the cross-border resource-oriented enterprises in recent years, a series of problems have been caused in the production process. Resource-oriented enterprises do not recognize the significant role of CSR in the development of enterprises, and do not incorporate CSR into the business management and strategic framework. Many sharp contradictions occur in the production process. At the same time, most local farmers and herdsmen lack the game weight compared to the enterprise. The interests of farmers and herdsmen have long been in an unequal position with the interests of enterprises. As a result, the local government, enterprises, and farmers and herdsmen cannot coordinate their interests and development concepts. The interests of farmers and herdsmen have been infringed, and the ecological environment has been destroyed. These are obvious loopholes of responsibility. In the long run, the accumulation of loopholes will inevitably affect the normal development of the society.

In the increasingly competitive economic environment, the economic model of the enterprise has changed from the previous simple model (investment-production-sales-profit) to the diversified environment. Corporate responsibility for society has become an obligation for enterprises. Although some resource-oriented enterprises have realized the necessity of social responsibility, and actively fulfilled their obligations, the lack of social responsibility is still the main feature of most resource-oriented enterprises in China. Although many companies have recognized the importance of CSR, they have not established an effective corporate culture based on social responsibility. Chinese enterprises have entered the market economy development-oriented enterprises from the most primitive capital accumulation enterprises, and the corporate culture still stays at the original stage of capital accumulation, with profit as the direction, all aiming at maximizing profits, and failing to establish social responsibility accurately. It ignores the problems of environmental protection and production safety, and even excessive pursuit of interests, which leads to the damage of the legitimate rights and interests of herders. There are also enterprises lacking integrity, malicious breach of contract, serious cases even ignoring the law, not taking any measures to protect the environment, and seriously polluting the environment. These series of phenomena reflect the lack of CSR awareness in China, and do not integrate CSR into corporate culture. The fulfillment of CSR requires the joint efforts of the government and the community.

3. Chinese companies' commitment to social responsibility stops at reactive social responsibility

Under the circumstance that China's relevant laws and regulations are not perfect, the subjective awareness of Chinese enterprises is not strong. Some enterprises neglect the implementation of social responsibility, such as ecological environmental protection and safe production. On the one hand, China's social responsibility practice activities started late. The sense of social responsibility has not yet penetrated the corporate culture; on the other hand, Chinese companies are extremely easy to focus on short-term economic benefits, always taking the maximum economic profit as the first goal, ignoring the long-term development of the enterprise, little attention is paid to environmental damage and public interests, and there is no sense to assume the corresponding social responsibilities. Therefore, in transnational operations, some contradictions and conflicts will inevitably arise in the local area. For example, in some regions and countries, conflicts between Chinese construction contractors and local communities have occurred in succession in recent years, which has had a significant impact on business operations. Therefore, the current commitment of resource-oriented enterprises to social responsibility is only reactive social responsibility. It is the passive performance of CSR. In subjective consciousness, they are unwilling to perform CSRs, that is, solutions will only be adopted when problems have already emerged, and feedback is available, in this way to recover the reputation of the company. In practice, it doesn't make much difference to fulfill the responsibility when the problem has already happened, which will only bring the enterprise into a desperate situation.

In the subjective consciousness of Chinese enterprises, the fulfillment of CSR only means the increase of enterprise costs and the reduction of profits. Enterprises believe that the protection of the ecological environment, the improvement of the working environment of employees, and the compensation of residents will cause the loss of corporate funds. To reduce the impact of production activities on the local ecology, resource-oriented enterprises upgrade the technology of mining and production and processing, such as the technical transformation of flue gas desulfurization, dust removal and boiler in the production process, and the reasonable handling of the coal grinding stone, fly ash and slag et. The introduction of these innovative technologies and new equipment will increase the production costs of enterprises and affect economic interests in the short term. In the initial stage of the development of China's market economy, the development of enterprises was not yet matured. Therefore, enterprises were more concerned with maximizing profits and minimizing costs, and there was little investment in society or the environment. The practice of CSR fulfillment was repeatedly failed. In addition, many cross-border enterprises are not aware of social responsibility in domestic production and management activities. They do not have good commitment to CSR, and there is no corresponding management mechanism in foreign production and management activities. As a result, the reputation of Chinese enterprises is damaged, and the economic interests of enterprises are also damaged.

On the government side, the input of social responsibility of resource-oriented enterprises has reduced the economic interests of enterprises. The reduction of profits will affect the overall growth of the local economy, and lead to the reduction of government tax revenue. The Chinese government lacks timely guidance on CSR implementation. Although the Chinese government has formulated relevant systems to require CSR behavior, in the process of institutional development of CSR reports, there has been a lack of effective guidance. Moreover, the Chinese government and relevant supervisory and administrative departments have not given effective attention to the research and implementation of environmental protection of enterprises, so in this case, it is difficult to manage CSR performance. Businesses and government parties often regard fulfilling social responsibility as a burden and have no internal motivation to fulfill their social responsibilities. At present, China's legislation on CSR still has certain flaws (Jie, 2015).

Article 5 of the current Company Law stipulates CSR as: a company engaged in business activities must abide by laws, practice theory and practice laws and regulations, abide by social morality, business ethics, be honest and trustworthy, accept the supervision of the government and the public, and assume social responsibility. A series of legal norms such as the Labor Law, the Consumer Protection Law and the Product Quality Law also reveal the intention of enterprises to assume social responsibility. Except for the CSR explicitly mentioned in the Company Law, other laws and regulations have not clearly defined the CSR. CSR, as stipulated in the Company Law, also lacks detailed operational rules, and there is no specific responsibility, making it impossible to effectively restrict corporate related behavior. Moreover, in the relevant laws and regulations on cross-border operation of Chinese enterprises, there is a lack of regulations and constraints on CSR. Therefore, cross-border enterprises have not yet established a long-term effective social responsibility management system. Even some enterprises that undertake lot of social responsibilities in China are still at the initial stage of exploration.

Some foreign companies with a high reputation for social responsibility have established a social responsibility management system that meets the requirements of the Social Responsibility Standard (SA8000). The SA8000 standard has become an internationally recognized CSR standard. It requires enterprises to undertake social responsibilities in the process of production and operation. There are minimum standards for specific issues such as the work environment, employee health and safety, employee training, wages, and trade union rights etc. Western countries have now perfectly integrated them with the corresponding production management system, while in China, the lack of such standards has led to constant friction between cross-border enterprises and local governments, enterprises, communities and employees.

Professor Michael Porter believes that only by strategically taking on social responsibilities, can companies exert the greatest positive impact on society, while at the same time harvesting the most lucrative business interests, and the advantages are more durable. For resource-oriented enterprises, accurately positioning enterprises to avoid blind implementation of social responsibility and engaging in strategic social responsibility is the only effective way to solve problems, prevent extreme contradictions, and enable enterprises to gain competitive advantage. To engage in strategic social responsibility, enterprises should, on one hand, understand the interrelationship between business and society from a more accurate perspective, that is, enterprises should not only focus on the contradictory relationship between business and society, and ignore the interdependence between them. On the other hand, enterprises need to combine the social responsibility they undertake with the specific strategies and plans of the company for comprehensive consideration. In Porter's view, companies should incorporate their social responsibilities into the corporate strategic framework, and carry out strategic social responsibilities, to exert the greatest positive impact on society, and reap the most lucrative commercial interests, and the social responsibility advantages will be more durable.

Strategic social responsibility guides companies to find value shared with other stakeholders, in their internal operations and social impact factors of the external competitive environment. The realization of this important task can not only correct the bias of enterprises and society towards each other, but also is an effective way to promote the coordinated development of enterprises and economy and society (Wang, 2013).

4. Possible disadvantages of the implementation of China's CSR standard system in transnational resource-oriented enterprises

First, it would increase the cost and reduce the benefits of resource-oriented enterprises. In the process of implementing the social responsibility mechanism, the improved enterprise's supervision and management will lead to the improvement of labor productivity and the coordinated development between various departments. Planned responsibilities among all departments and employees will greatly improve the overall management level of the company, which is mainly reflected in the substantial increase in productivity, and the enhancement of coordination and planning among all departments. The staff turnover rate is greatly reduced, which strengthens the cohesion of the enterprise. Employees' working hours are becoming more reasonable, and their mental outlook will be greatly improved. The company adopts skill-based compensation, and the income of employees with high skills will be greatly improved. The stability of these employees will also be greatly improved, and the loss of employees will gradually decrease, which will help attract more excellent employees. The flexibility of communication channels allows employees to have channels for expressing opinions and suggestions, so that employees can appreciate the company's respect for their personality and value, improve their communication skills, and increase their sense of professional safety and belonging. After the stability of employees increases, the company's employment costs will be decreased, employees' mobility will be decreased, and maturity will be increased. The cost of loss, due to the mistake of new employee and the turnover of old and new employee, will be greatly reduced. Therefore, many coal companies are reluctant to implement the standard system of CSR. However, the implementation of the standard system of CSR is meaningful to the long-term interests of enterprises.

Second, Chinese companies' social responsibility is not well understood. Li Ma and Shanhong Qi believe that CSR is a concept closely related to management ethics. The conflict and balance of corporate profit goals and social interest goals is the starting point and destination of the theory of CSR. Wenmei Guo and Youhuan Li also believe that as a responsible enterprise, it is not only for profit, but also for the interests of stakeholders, such as providing consumers with reliable and safe products, establishing good cooperative relations with business partners, paying more attention to environmental and social welfare undertakings, and these are in line with the requirements for achieving sustainable development of society. The profitability of the enterprise is destined for the company to pursue profit maximization as its main goal. Similarly, the sociality of the enterprise is also determined to be responsible for fulfilling its social responsibility. When enterprises fulfill their social responsibilities, the cost will inevitably increase. Enterprises should regard this as an investment behavior, because in the long run, enterprises can increase their competitiveness by fulfilling their social responsibilities. The implementation of the standard system of CSR clearly stipulates that coal enterprises fulfill their social responsibilities to employers.

Corporate social responsibility is conducive to the creation of a broader living environment, such as improving employees' sense of responsibility, initiative and creativity, helping the production activities to be carried out in a safe and orderly manner, giving decision makers and operators greater flexibility. It helps to gain the trust of the government, and thus get more government funding and preferential policies. At the same time, corporate assuming social responsibility is a long-term management method, a form of advertising that attracts customers for a long time, so that many customers can be obtained in a long-term and stable manner. All of this creates conditions for the sustainable development of the company.

The pace of transnational operations of Chinese enterprises has accelerated, and foreign investment and cooperation have developed rapidly. They play a very important role in maintaining growth, stabilizing external demand, adjusting structure and promoting the development of China's business. They have become an important driving force for China's open economy. Strengthening the social responsibility of enterprises has become an issue that Chinese enterprises must face in the process of transnational operations and is an effective way to achieve their own sustainable development. It can be said that whether we are willing or not, the issue of CSR has been closely linked to international trade issues and has become a problem that Chinese enterprises must pay attention to when entering the world market. In the context of globalization, strengthening and enhancing the sense of social responsibility of transnational corporations is not only an issue that China cannot avoid in entering the international market, but also an inevitable choice for China to build a socialist harmonious society and achieve sustainable economic development.

5. Mongolia's domestic legal environment is unstable

Mongolia's domestic legal environment is unstable, the legal form is diverse but extensive and simple, lack of overall planning, guidance and prospective seriousness, and the policy environment is greatly affected by political factors, etc., which will also affect the CSR implementation of Chinese enterprises in Mongolia. In such a sovereign state, citizens of the country have the right to know what decisions are made about the exploitation of natural resources, the government's share of mining companies and how it is spent on mining revenue. However, compared with other forms of economic activity, the mining industry is largely in remote areas, and most of the mining income detail is not clear to the people. Thus, without proper regulation, it is possible that important mining decisions cannot be controlled and leads to corruption and mismanagement. Mongolia is also improving related issues, suggesting that mining income be allocated through local funds and local development funds. According to the law, 25% internal value-added tax, 5% mining royalties, 30% oil use fees, local governments must first transfer the money to the local development fund, and then redistributed according to regional conditions, including population density, local scale, development standards and tax incentives. Due to the serious lag in the formulation of the legal system in Mongolia, It is often when a problem has occurred, or an event has occurred, that rules are established to constrain it. The serious lack of foresight and guidance makes Mongolia's laws and regulations only serve as a punisher. All of these have greatly reduced the effectiveness of CSR implementation and greatly reduced operability. Court participation is small and late. The court's supervision of CSR will only be investigated if the problem has been clarified and the loss has already been caused. Moreover, the court's lawsuit must go through a series of complicated procedures, with very weak timeliness.

In the past decade, some important laws on anti-corruption, transparency and accountability, for example the Audit Law proposed in 2015, have been adopted. In addition, in the documents about the environmental impacts on related resource extraction, some important supplementary mining local modules, such as mining cadaster systems, also show relevant environmental factors. The mining industry and investors, in the past few years, are directly related to laws and regulations. However, there are differences between the changes in the law and the reality. The Mongolian mining industry provides information for the dissemination of information, lack of transparency, and the credibility of information held by governments and mining companies is very low. Originally, government agencies, public and private companies can provide a lot of information, but all citizens, participants, investors and local communities do not know the truth. Only strict behavioral control is a powerful barrier to corruption, and a mechanism to improve business performance at all levels of government. And only Countries that have current and future government goals will be aware of the future benefits of national natural resource management strategies.

6. Mongolia has insufficient supervision over the CSR implementation

The public and social opinions have insufficient supervision over the publication of CSR reports. It is far from enough to rely solely on the binding force of laws and regulations to urge enterprises to fulfill their CSR and publish their CSR reports. A single regulation cannot form a driving force for companies to publish relevant environmental information. The public's concern for the environment and the necessary public pressure are important external drivers for companies to fulfill their social responsibilities. The environmental awareness of the public society is still very weak, and it is of great practical significance to raise the attention of Chinese public and social opinions on CSR.

At present, the focus of the Mongolian government is more inclined to the development of enterprises and economic interests. The emphasis on the supervision of CSR is insufficient, and there is no effective monitoring system. The society does not have a special platform and organization to disclose and evaluate the implementation of corporate social responsibility. The media's attention and propaganda are far from enough. There is no public opinion guidance to supervise enterprises. Therefore, the implementation of social responsibility of resource-oriented enterprises is often not well supervised and guided, and it further aggravates the lack of motivation for enterprises to fulfill their responsibilities. The evaluation of social responsibility and environmental responsibility lacks a unified and standardized indicator evaluation system. Each enterprise has different contents for fulfilling social and environmental responsibilities, which is not conducive to comparison and evaluation among enterprises. Moreover, the content of social responsibility and environmental responsibility has not been reviewed by a third party, and the authenticity of the information and data cannot be determined. The content disclosed is also determined by the enterprise itself. The company can selectively disclose only positive social responsibility information. This lack of environmental and social responsibility evaluation system hinders the realization of corporate social responsibility.

Compared with the US multi-channel supervision model, Mongolia has very few channels of supervision over CSR. For example, for listed companies, only the CSRC (China Securities Regulatory Commission) is really required to provide real information. For other types of enterprises, the supervision mechanism is more incomplete, and can only be supervised by government administrative agencies and limited written laws and a few responsible media. Nor has it given full play to the supervisory role of consumers in enterprises but has always protected them as a vulnerable group. Therefore, Mongolia's supervision of CSR is lack of intensity. Only when the whole society participates together and let the behavior of enterprises always under the attention of the society, will the CSR be better implemented.

Chapter 4

CSR Mechanism Construction of Transnational Resource-oriented Enterprises in CMEC

With the pace of CMEC construction accelerating in recent years, China's resource-oriented enterprises have made frequent foreign investments. However, a series of problems have emerged. There are contradictions between enterprises and residents, investment interests are not protected, vicious accidents occur frequently, and the interests of employees and local residents are insufficiently protected. This series of problems will affect the image of China's resource-oriented enterprises and reduce the resources of China's resource-oriented enterprises. Competitiveness has seriously restricted and hindered the sustainable development of China's foreign investment enterprises. Therefore, resource-oriented enterprises should pay more attention to the social impact brought by the host country, while pursuing economic benefits. Because the enterprise is essentially an organization influenced by various markets and society, it is the link of the relationship between stakeholders. Therefore, more social responsibilities should be undertaken, such as energy conservation and emission reduction, safety and environmental protection, and human rights protection, to achieve common economic and social development. In addition to government agencies and various functional departments, the governance of social responsibility of transnational resource-oriented enterprises requires the active participation of enterprises, society, international organizations and host countries, and achieves a new equilibrium, that is, synergy between them. Therefore, building a social responsibility coordination promotion mechanism for transnational resource-oriented enterprises is an important link for China's foreign investment resource-oriented enterprises to achieve sustainable development.

4.1 TheMain Body of SR Synergy of Resource-oriented Enterprises in CMEC

With the continuous development of corporate management concepts, the relationship between enterprises and their stakeholders has shifted from opposition to unity. As a result, stakeholders, related to the daily activities of transnational resource-oriented enterprises, have become the key to the coordinated promotion of their social responsibility. From the internal and external analysis of the enterprise, the main body of the social responsibility synergy of transnational resource-oriented enterprises is defined as follows:

1. Transnational resource-oriented enterprise

According to the classical economics view, the primary goal of the enterprise is to maximize the economic benefits. As the relationship between the enterprise and the society becomes more and more close, the position of socialization in the enterprise becomes more and more prominent, and social problems have become more and more important in enterprises. As an economic organization, transnational corporations are understandable to run after profit, but their social responsibility fulfillment has been questioned. Some people believe that fulfilling social responsibilities will reduce the economic benefits of enterprises and create a difference with the costs of competitors. However, the failure of enterprises to generate trust will create a crisis of trust in the public and cause more serious losses. The most typical example is the melamine incident of Sanlu Group in 2008. The company's irresponsible behavior towards the society not only caused the company to suffer heavy losses, but also the Chinese dairy industry suffered a serious blow. Many countries did not allow Chinese dairy products to be exported. Therefore, while Sanlu Group does not strictly fulfill its social responsibilities, it cannot guarantee the maximum benefit of the company. This event result is consistent with the conclusions reached by Klein and Dawar, when they studied the evaluation of CSR on consumer attribution in the context of product crisis. That is, the deficient performance of CSR will affect consumers' brand evaluation and purchase intention. Transnational corporations face a conflict of interest dilemma: minimizing operating costs; and recognizing governance regimes can increase costs.

Critics also pointed out that other factors also constrain the ability of corporate governance. First, there is no effective mechanism to comment and urge companies to assume social responsibility. While shareholders can and occasionally improve corporate social responsibility performance, they prefer to abandon their social responsibilities for financial gain. Second, transnational corporations do not have the knowledge and skills which are necessary to complete social responsibility governance. Third, the company lacks the motivation to collectively manage CSR. In general, companies are reluctant to actively participate in the governance of CSR, because participation in CSR governance will increase the cost of business operations, unless it knows that other companies are also involved in governance and have resulted in the same cost. The lack of power and obligation, especially the lack of public management knowledge and collective action issues, greatly limit the ability of the private sectors to participate in global CSR governance. Clearly, the ability of the private sectors to individually participate in global CSR governance is seriously inadequate.

2. Host country

The host country is the first major entity in the external environment for the synergy of social responsibility of transnational resource-oriented enterprises. It plays a supervisory and driving role in the entire process of fulfilling social responsibility of enterprises. By formulating rules and systems to constrain enterprises, enterprises must Act in accordance with government regulations. The expectation of social performance of transnational corporations is the core of modern state adjustment. There is no doubt that every country wants to retain the privilege of choosing labor, the environment and wage standards. Among these stakeholders, the government has the strongest authority and the institutional capacity to enforce expectations in the country. However, under the pressure of a huge global economy, this may force the government to adopt lower regulatory standards, because high regulatory policies have the risk of preventing foreign investment from entering. While the state wants to promote global standards of CSR, any successful process needs to improve competitive pressures, and increase the leverage they engage with investment companies. In addition, the national government has another shortcoming, that is, official corruption, or corporate bribery of officials, leads to the failure of effective governance of CSR.

3. Home country

In the process of development and implementation of resource-oriented corporate social responsibility for foreign investment, the home government shall give full play to the role of supervision, assistance and promotion, promote the fulfillment of social responsibility of foreign-invested resource-oriented enterprises, and help solve problems in the CSR implementation process. Since China is in the period of social and economic transformation, the understanding and implementation of social responsibility by resource-oriented enterprises is not enough. The government should promote the social responsibility construction of resource-oriented enterprises from the legal level. Promoting the legalization of social responsibility of transnational resource-oriented enterprises can enable resource-oriented enterprises to write social responsibility into the company's articles of association and become a system that is more conducive to their implementation abroad. When resource-oriented enterprises in China fulfill their social responsibilities abroad, there may be situations in which social responsibility is not fulfilled to maximizing short-term benefits. At this time, the government of the home country is required to give certain intervention and supervision. Only in this way can the sustainable development of enterprises be guaranteed and lay a good foundation for the smooth implementation of national energy strategy.

4. Inter-governmental international organization

An intergovernmental international organization is a national alliance or a national consortium of more than two countries. The alliance was established by its member governments, through an agreement in accordance with international law, and has a permanent system or a set of institutions. Its purpose is, relying on cooperation among member states, to seek the goal of meeting common interests. Famous international organizations include the World Trade Organization (WTO), the International Monetary Fund (IMF) and the World Bank (WB) etc. Compared with the private sectors, intergovernmental international organizations have the advantage of power and institutional capacity. The power comes from the members (countries) who participate in these organizations.

Another advantage is institutional capacity. Countries participating in these organizations believe that organizations can play a role in maintaining world peace and promote world economic development. It is undeniable that intergovernmental international organizations have achieved a certain independent status, with power, investment and trusteeship granted by member states. Because of this, it also means that there are two shortcomings in inter-governmental international organizations. First is that the issues of concern to international organizations are all issues that governments consider important. Intergovernmental international organizations often have to consider from the standpoint of member states when dealing with international affairs. Second, international organizations have succeeded in cultivating economic liberalization, and have also led to increased calls for improving social issues and the establishment of a new economic liberalization. For example, the World Trade Organization is called upon to use trade policies to encourage countries to adopt stronger measures to protect intellectual property rights and raise workers' wages and environmental standards. International labor standards are proposed by the International Labor Organization (ILO), but the World Trade Organization is required to adopt the labor standards, because the World Trade Organization has potential international trade penalties. This appeal was often rejected by the World Trade Organization. World trade organization officials say the organization's prerogatives need to be used with caution when dealing with international affairs.

Skeptics believe that trade or financial liberalization policies will prompt governments to enact regulatory policies that will be followed by more developing countries. Instead, they advocate that public responsibilities related to environmental, health and labor standards should be borne by national governments. This appeal continues and has not been resolved. Inter-governmental international organizations value the interests of all countries and undermine the interests of the non-governmental sectors. They do not have institutional advantages that focus on CSR issues, but can only express concerns about these issues through trade and investment.

5. Civil society

Civil society refers to the sum of all civil organizations and civil relations outside the state or government. It is a non-mandatory action group that revolves around common interests, goals, and values, including non-governmental organizations, voluntary associations of citizens, communities, associations, interest groups, and sports organized by citizens. It usually operates in charities, non-governmental organizations, community organizations, women's organizations, religious groups, professional associations, trade unions, self-help organizations, social movement groups, business associations, alliances, etc. Although civil society does not occupy the advantages of wealth and power, it cares for the disadvantaged groups, and has the natural talent of social mobilization and social advocacy. It is the most active driving force in social responsibility governance. The power of civil society comes from the inflammatory messages they spread, which may lead to a strong public protest. This kind of protest has truly affected the public's buying behavior and may even affect their vote on goods.

Civil society exists in different countries, but they are united for a common theme. They believe that this demand is more likely to attract everyone's attention than election officials or business managers. Their impact on governance is considerable. They have succeeded in making everyone aware of the negative benefits of globalization and forced corporate managers to respond. Governments and companies have realized that the capacity of civil society cannot be underestimated.

Radical groups in civil society continue to inspire other members to join, and existing members are doing their best to fight for organizational goals. These efforts have transformed social dynamics into political influences. However, this concern in civil society also has weaknesses. Most importantly, radical groups have created problems related to obligations. The demands they make come from their own small scope, not the needs of the majority, which means that their expectations of the government and the business are often unrealistic, too idealistic, and out of touch with reality. This radical strategy of the radical group can affect the public's point of view, making the public not have the patience to accept the more advanced views of the institutional forum. These factors affect their ability to be in a neutral, objective position when setting CSR expectations.

As mentioned above, a comprehensive overview of the multi-resource-oriented corporate CSAR promotion mechanism is carried out by various stakeholders, and the degree of closeness of each stakeholder and enterprise development is not the same. This research is not to solve the problem of CSR, but to mobilize the forces of the international community to promote CSR by constructing a mechanism for the synergy of SR of transnational resource-oriented enterprises from a macro perspective. This research is based on the close relationship between the company and internal and external stakeholders and classifies the importance of the impact of corporate social responsibility. From the macro perspective, the main body of CSR synergy of resource-oriented enterprises in CMEC is divided into three categories: transnational resource-oriented enterprises, host countries and society.

Transnational resource-oriented enterprises mainly refer to many stakeholders closely related to the development of enterprises, including shareholders, employees, consumers, suppliers and competitors. The participation of these stakeholders is a favorable support for the sustainable development of the company. Whether the company actively fulfills its social responsibility will affect their development. Therefore, they are risk-sharing partners. It should be emphasized that enterprises are not only the direct subject of the coordinated promotion of social responsibility, but also the indirect subject of the government and society to promote the role of CSR. In today's rapid economic development, the social structure has undergone profound changes. Enterprises have more social resources. Enterprises play an important role in the entire social economy and are vital to the harmonious development of society.

The host country refers to the country and region where the company conducts transnational business cooperation. The host country can control and intervene in the enterprise, and at the same time it has certain economic strength. However, the host country often faces a dilemma when it supervises and controls the performance of the social responsibility of transnational corporations. On the one hand, the host country will formulate lofty standards of social responsibility management and control policies based on the needs of its own resources, environment and social development. On the other hand, high social responsibility management and control policies will increase the cost of foreign investment, reduce the willingness of foreign companies to enter, and affect the international development of the domestic economy.

Society mainly refers to the network of relationships. Here it refers to other stakeholders, such as home countries, international organizations, non-governmental organizations (NGOs), which have an impact on the production and management activities of enterprises, other than enterprises and host countries. Some scholars believe that society has three interrelated internal foundations. First are ideas and beliefs. Ideas include attitudes and consciousness. It is with ideas that a wide range of life goals are established. We believe we exist in a good living environment. Second is the system. The system means that the society establishes a way of doing things in line with the consensus, such as the enterprise system, the political system, the legal system, etc. The third is the material basis, which is a tangible form of matter, such as land, minerals, and machinery. The combination of these three intrinsic foundations has emerged as a defined society.

Although the host country government and society are both the main body of transnational resource-oriented enterprises' CSR promotion, their functions are different. First, the leading role of the host government is to supervise and guide, and to promote CSR through legislation and policies. The society mainly promotes CSR through public opinion and evaluation mechanisms. Both indirectly affect the production and business activities of the enterprise. In the process of continuous development of social responsibility, the host country and society have become the main body of the CSR synergy of important transnational enterprises.

4.2 Motivation Analysis of Each Entity to Promote CSR

1. The motivation of transnational resource-oriented enterprises to actively fulfill their social responsibilities

Enterprises are the internal subjects of fulfilling social responsibilities. Most scholars believe that the reason why enterprises actively perform social responsibilities is because of the interdependence between social responsibility and profit. Enterprises can fulfill their social responsibilities and benefit the interests of all parties. Relevant people can benefit from it, and the company also benefits from it. From this, enterprises fulfill their social responsibilities due to their own profit-driven nature. In general, the motivation for transnational corporations to consciously fulfill their social responsibilities is to improve economic efficiency, to defend, and due to the host country pressure.

(1) Improve economic efficiency

Transnational corporations can improve their economic efficiency by assuming social responsibilities, which can be analyzed from the following aspects.

First, on the surface, it seems that transnational corporations will sacrifice some of their current interests by assuming social responsibility. On the contrary, the financial performance of transnational companies will be upgraded to varying degrees due to social responsibility. Take the example of 100 "S&P500" and "Best Corporate Citizens" selected by American Business Ethics magazine. Based on 1-3 years of overall return, sales growth rate and profit growth rate, as well as the net profit margin and return on equity, the overall financial situation of the "S&P 500" is far worse than that of "Best Corporate Citizen" companies. The average score of the latter is 10 percentage points higher than the average of the former.

Second, transnational companies taking on social responsibility can help reduce operating cost and increase efficiency. If transnational corporations play a corresponding social responsibility to save energy, protect the environment, eliminate the gap between the rich and the poor, and improve the quality of human life in transnational operations, they can reduce or avoid criticism, limitation and punishment from government departments, public interest groups and the public. In this way, normal production and operation activities can be guaranteed without interference, and even the corporate would be praised and rewarded by the government and the public. Meanwhile, they can enjoy preferential policies such as preferential supply of raw materials and exemption of inspection of products.

Third, transnational corporation taking on social responsibilities can also improve resource utilization. If a transnational company considers fulfilling its social responsibilities in the process of making global business decisions, it will take active measures to promote the development of circular economy, improve the comprehensive development of resources and recovery, and form a benign production process with higher resource productivity and lower pollution emission rate. It can effectively save resources for the society and reduce the operating costs of the enterprise.

(2) Defense

Defense mainly refers to the relationship between the company and its competitors. The market competition in the whole industry is fierce. Once a company successfully fulfills its social responsibilities, the competitors will be in the defensive purpose to actively fulfill the same social responsibilities. Although the price, quality and design are still the decisive factors restricting the transaction between enterprises and customers, the brand and image of the company are also important forces that determine the purchasing power of consumers. So, if the company does not do this, customers may prefer companies with better brands and image. According to Edelman's 2010 "Good Intentions" research report, consumers in emerging market countries prefer brands that are passionate about public welfare. Therefore, a new P (Purpose) has been added to the traditional marketing "4P" (Product, Price, Place, and Promotion).

In addition, under the trend of economic globalization, there are basically no "remote areas" in the world. Enterprises are in the international market competition, and CSR has become an important indicator for measuring the capabilities of enterprises in the world. This can be seen in numerous international CSR campaigns and international CSR performance indicator systems. Transnational corporations use social responsibility to advertise their uniqueness and convey their social ideas to customers. For the sake of defense and competition, Chinese enterprises must keep up with the trend of the times and strive to create more competitive advantages by fulfilling their social responsibilities and maintaining their competitive position and advantages. Especially for resource-oriented enterprises, their own characteristics of "taking from nature" require that they must be able to give back to nature, to meet the social expectations of enterprise development, gain a good reputation, and not to cause dissatisfaction of the masses. In this way, the corporate can gain a foothold in the industry and maintain a lasting competitive advantage.

(3) Host country pressure

By investing in host countries with their own monopolistic advantages and competitive advantages, transnational companies can make more use of the host country's social resources (such as labor, capital and raw materials) to obtain more profits than in the home country. What's more, it can solve the bottleneck problem of resources in the home country. To a certain extent, investments by transnational corporations in host countries have an impact on host country sovereignty, local culture and the natural environment. As a sovereign state, the involvement of transnational corporations will increase the management difficulty. Even some scholars believe that economic globalization related to transnational corporations will be used as a new way of colonialism to usurp the host country's sovereignty. The transnational corporations' influence on local culture can be two-sided. On the one hand, more and more transnational companies invest in host countries. It will promote cultural exchanges and local cultural prosperity. On the other hand, many investments by transnational corporations can have a negative impact on the culture of the host country. This will not only bring social problems but also serious political problems. There are also environmental impacts. Many of the plans of transnational corporations cannot be implemented due to restrictions on the resources and environment of the home country but can be realized in the host country. Through investment, the resource and environmental issues are transferred to the host country, which in turn affects the health and economic sustainability of the host country. Therefore, whether from the perspective of economy, ethics or responsibility, transnational corporations, owning large market share and profits, have the responsibility and obligation to actively compensate the host country society.

The existence of transnational corporations has a good effect on the economic development of the host country, but it may also have a serious negative impact on the local economic development. Governments in many countries have taken more active actions to further strengthen international cooperation, to maintain effective monitoring of the behavior of transnational corporations. In response to the anti-competitive behavior of transnational corporations' restrictive business practices, many developed countries, and more and more developing countries, have enacted corresponding competition legislation, prohibiting restrictive horizontal agreements, acquiring and abusing dominance, and anti-competitive behaviors such as large-scale restrictive vertical distribution agreements, hoping to promote competition through competition policies, and to achieve optimal allocation of resources. The mergers and acquisitions (M&A) activities of transnational corporations are likely to cause market privilege or control status of a small number of enterprises. Many countries have added supplementary clauses on M&A in the competition law, so that the scope of M&A activities is also governed by separate legislation.

2. The motivation of host country to promote CSR

The social performance expectation of transnational corporations is the core of modern state adjustment. There is no doubt that every country wants to retain the privilege of choosing between Labor, the environment and wage standards. Among these stakeholders, the government has the strongest authority and the institutional capacity to enforce expectations domestically. However, under the pressure of the global economy, the host government may be forced to adopt lower regulatory standards, because high regulatory policies have the risk of preventing FDI from entering. In addition, the host government has another shortcoming, that is, official corruption or corporate bribe, which has led to the failure to successfully manage CSR. However, based on the long-term interests of the people and economic development of the country, the host country government must act as a constitutor, promoter, and supervisor in the process of promoting the social responsibility of transnational enterprises.

(1) Constitutor

Due to the internal and externalities of market failures, enterprises have a need for government regulation. Government regulation is a government or a country that adopts corrective measures and behavioral restrictions when corporate behavior and social common goals are inconsistent. To give enterprises a good market environment, the government regulates in it. Therefore, the government assumes the role of a constitutor in the development of CSR. The government formulates relevant policies and regulations and establishes technical standards to encourage enterprises to fulfill their CSR.

(2) Promoter

As a promoter, the government mainly carries out propaganda, education, advocacy and responsibility research through administrative resources, and through its own advantages and status. It pays attention to cultivating the consciousness of CSR and improving the level of CSR. In addition, through government procurement and other measures, it gives financial incentives to the implementation of good enterprises, guide the flow of CSR investment, and encourage enterprises to actively fulfill their social responsibilities. Through a series of measures, the government fundamentally enables enterprises to establish awareness, and regard social responsibility as the basic activities of enterprises.

(3) Supervisor

As the government itself is authoritative, it can supervise the implementation of CSR by issuing laws and regulations that are mandatory and binding, using administrative means, auditing and certification. China is in the primary stage of socialism. If the cost of a lack of CSR is much lower than its income, the enterprise will not consciously contact social responsibility, and the whole society will have the phenomenon of "bad money expelling good money". Therefore, it is necessary to increase the supervision and punishment of acts that harm social interests, which is also the role of the government as supervisor.

3. The motivation of the society to promote CSR

Society is a collection of people and people. It is a collection of complex social relationships. Different social subjects have different goals. For example, environmental organizations are focused on global environmental protection, and labor organizations aim to safeguard the legitimate rights and interests of workers. But in general, the goals of various social organizations are for the sustainable development of human society, so the goals of different social organizations are the same. Therefore, social organizations, with their non-profit nature, have become an important force in regulating the normal operation of society. Specifically, the media and international organizations are representative and influential organizations in this area.

The media is the medium for the effective communication of CRS in the society. Through the dissemination of the media, people from all walks of life have paid great attention to social responsibility. It also has an important impact on decision makers in enterprises. The media also gives decision-makers the opportunity to disseminate information through their own attributes. That is, the decision-makers can use the media platform to publicly discuss policy issues, such as social security systems, CSR and other issues of public concern. The government can also adjust and coordinate relevant policies based on the feedback from the media, to understand the stakeholders' plans and action strategies. Similarly, for Mongolia, the media plays the same role in all relevant national interest groups, by summarizing and disseminating information, in this way to coordinate actions of various stakeholder groups and make the resource-oriented enterprises of the two countries take up social responsibilities. The media has become an important medium for the society to pay attention to the CSR fulfillment.

In fact, as far as CSR is concerned, the media is not only a medium for disseminating information, but also an important stakeholder of the company. From a certain perspective, the media is a society, and the media can mobilize public opinion to approve, oppose, mobilize, promote or terminate corporate behavior, including social responsibility behavior. The media provides good news to the society, especially the various stakeholders of the company. They adjust their participation in the entire system based on the content of the news, which in turn affects the survival and development of the company. Therefore, in real life, companies are often willing to choose social issues that are likely to cause media attention to fulfill social responsibilities, such as sponsorship education or charity. The disgraceful behavior of enterprises is often corrected after exposure through the media. Enterprises regain their reputation by taking certain social responsibility actions.

The most profound change in the 21st century is economic globalization. With the increasing influence of transnational corporations on the economic, political and social culture of various countries, CSR has gradually become the focus of international attention. To unify the standards and rules of CSR, international organizations have played their due role. At present, there are more than 400 similar standards in the world. These standards make social responsibility more specific and become a concrete quantitative indicator of operational measurement. Social responsibility standards are becoming a valuable tool and means to promote CSR.

The main sign of the formal involvement of the United Nations in CSR issues is the Global Compact program, which was introduced in January 1999. The core of the plan is to require companies to comply with, support and implement a set of 10 basic principles in human rights, labor standards, the environment and anti-corruption within their respective spheres of influence, and by building socially responsible and creative business models to build a global framework to promote sustainable growth and social efficiency. In *The Guide for Transnational Enterprises* established by the Organization for Economic Co-operation and Development, it confirms some of the basic social responsibilities that transnational corporations should undertake.

The International Labor Organization (ILO) is a tripartite organization of governments, employers' organizations and trade unions. The organization has developed a series of conventions that form international labor standards. The eight conventions on the basic rights of workers, such as association freedom, collective bargaining, forced labor, child labor, and employment discrimination, are called basic or core conventions. And there are also important conventions on working hours and rest periods, wages, social security, occupational safety and health. In addition, other relevant international organizations have also developed some CSR standards, such as the Global Reporting Initiative and the World Bank's Social Responsibility Standards, etc.

4.3 Comparison of CSR Synergy Mechanism and Other Promotion Modes

This part mainly studies the CRS synergy mechanism, compares it with the traditional single promotion method, and finds the defects of the single method by studying from a single perspective. Finally, it is determined to solve the problem through tripartite coordinated promotion.

4.3.1 Business, Government, and Society: The Defects of Looking from Single Perspective

1. The Neo-Liberalism School dominated by enterprise and its shortcomings

The theoretical basis of Neo-Liberalism School can be obtained from the aforementioned instrumental theory. The school believes that the adoption of CSR by companies is rational and profitable in the long run. The performance of CSR is not simply equivalent to the charity of the company. Because the benefits of CSR fulfillment by various departments of the enterprise are far greater than the tax reduction benefits of the company engaged in charitable acts. In all markets, corporations are always motivated by risk and reward. Through CSR strategic management, the company obtains various corresponding CSR certificates. CSR policies such as social investment will attract more product demand and various production factors for enterprises, such as labor and capital. The neoliberal risk-reward, as a motivational mechanism for CSR, seems plausible on the surface, however, it ignores that CSR will lead to disorder of internal resource allocation and distortion of economic incentive mechanism.

First, the company must set up the necessary CSR execution department to spend a certain amount of time on the CSR. As a result, the time and resource allocation of enterprise management are misplaced, and these are the essence of the market function. If the company's CSR implementation is completely in accordance with market signals, then CSR activities will be reflected in the rational use of the necessary methods to analyze the needs of society, but now many CSR activities have obvious political motives. This is determined by the public relations of existing businesses and society. Even though we assume that social needs are effectively identified and prioritized, but many CSR activities also involve significant transaction costs. For example, establishing CSR guidelines requires a lot of time and money to explain and use them. Second, CSR will distort resource allocation at the microeconomic level, leading to distorted prices and judgments on supply and demand. Third, the politicization of corporate organizations can also lead to distortions in resource allocation. The stakeholder model politicizes the organization from two perspectives. At the management level, the stakeholder board will introduce a series of politicized representatives of stakeholders; at the operational level, some degree of CSR guidance rules lead to the emergence of non-productive behavior.

2. Government-led CSR and defects

The theoretical basis of government-led is the normative theory. Government-led advocates believe that policy makers should actively promote the establishment and strengthening of binding mechanisms for enterprises. For the government, CSR is closely related to it, so it should be taken proactively. However, the government may have defects in leading CSR. First, there are issues related to government failures such as politicization, bureaucratization, and inefficiency. Secondly, the government represents its own national enterprise in the international environment. Therefore, whether it is a poor country or a rich country, the pressure on enterprises to fulfill CSR will consider the interests of their enterprises, resulting in reduced pressure.

The government-led surface has created a new era of cooperation between the private sector and the public regulation sector to promote CSR. In fact, there is a confrontation between the government and the enterprise under this rhetoric. First, CSR does not simply represent possible regulation. CSR is a field of power claims and expansion. Since CSR fulfillment must be decided by the company, CSR gives the enterprise the right to make policy decisions. To some extent, companies have transcended democratically elected governments, which may result in a lack of democracy and responsibility. Second, although the participation of a certain number of stakeholders is beneficial, corporate participation in policy development in the context of CSR reflects a general shift in power between companies and governments. In the CSR field, different governments and enterprises are in the struggles of "occupation" and "retreat". Third, in the international arena, CSR is the field of political claims. The development of increasingly sophisticated CSR provisions demonstrates the transfer of power from nation-states to international organizations and transnational corporations. In the worst sense, this is the national state's transfer of management power to domestic corporations.

3. Socially dominant CSR and defects

Society, as the promoter of the CSR movement, has different goals, strategies, methods, and organizational forms. It can be said that the entire NGO community is like an NGO society, and there are many different viewpoints and methods within. From the perspective of NGO strategies, they can be divided into two categories: participation and confrontation. Before the 1970s, the general view was that the responsibility of enterprises was to increase the profits of investors and shareholders. After the 1970s, with the outbreak of a series of corporate scandals, companies could not commit fraudulent bribery in order to seek profits, and enterprises could not interfere with the political affairs of the host country. These views were generally accepted by the society. After entering the 1980s, with the exposure of a series of environmental incidents, the CSR movement had been unprecedentedly high. NGOs recognized the damage caused by transnational companies to the environment, and transnational companies must take measures in their environmental protection. Therefore, NGOs strongly advocated that enterprises should perform social responsibilities. Since the early 1990s, the Non-Governmental Organizations of Human Rights Organizations have called for transnational corporations to take more responsibility in promoting labor rights, human rights, social justice, and sustainable development. At present, NGOs are committed to persuading companies to accept various regulations, to regulate corporate behavior in protecting labor rights, human rights, and the environment. Those who advocate conscious CSR methods believe that corporate behavior must meet the three bottom lines, respectively economic responsibility, environmental responsibility and social responsibility, and encourage enterprises to consciously adopt various new ethical standards.

However, the conscious CSR method is not the only strategy for government organizations. In the field of NGOs, there is another view, considering that as a product of institutional arrangements, transnational corporations cannot consciously fulfill their social responsibilities. Only through economic methods or resorting to binding laws can companies be more responsible to society. Those who hold this view are hoping to set off a mass social movement, forcing the government to implement strong domestic and international legal standards, so that transnational corporations can assume social responsibility. The second is to seek cooperation from the trade unions, form alliances with the labor organizations, and maintain the rights and interests of workers through collective bargaining and pressure. Many NGOs see strong legal standards as their goal. However, they also believe that many large transnational companies adopt conscious CSR standards on a large scale, which is the only way to achieve the goal of strong legal standards. However, some other NGOs regard the conscious CSR standard as a manifestation of the public relations of transnational corporations and are a substitute for severe legal constraints. Even some NGOs regard the conscious CSR standard as the image propaganda of transnational corporations and are the means to evade government legal constraints.

The Non-Governmental Organizations that advocate participation in cooperation believe that it is advisable to impose strong legal constraints on transnational corporations, but it is preferable to consciously adopt CSR standards, because for now and in the near future, strong laws are not easy to achieve. At this stage, it will only be fiercely opposed if transnational corporations are required to abandon their right of movement freedom and succumb to strong laws. Transnational corporations are performing CSR not for fear of coercive tactics of NGOs, but to maintain the company's reputation, and are feared that the stock price would fall. Just as Shell Company tried to sink the abandoned large oil floating reserve into the 6,000-foot-deep seabed in the North Atlantic in the summer of 1995, it was strongly resisted by some radical environmental NGOs, forcing Shell to abandon the decision. Although it is impossible to deny the key role of NGOs in the boycott movement, Shell gave up the decision because it was afraid of the ethical condemnation, and fear that the stock would fall. Finally, it made commitment to fulfilling CSR. The conscious CSR approach is not a substitute for an enforceable legal standard, but a complement to it. Because the establishment of an enforceable legal standards system in the future still relies, to a considerable extent, on the company's monitoring of its own behavior.

4.3.2 Solution: Dynamic Coordination of the Host Government, Transnational corporations and Society

To truly achieve the change of perspective, we must first understand the current situation of transnational enterprises, host government and society. Judging from the reality, the three parties are currently in an unbalanced state. Host governments and societies are quite proactive, they make demands and expectations for transnational corporations, stipulate legal obligations, and transfer social responsibility pressures to enterprises. Transnational corporations are the direct subject of assuming social responsibility pressure and solving social responsibility issues, and they are the focus of all parties.

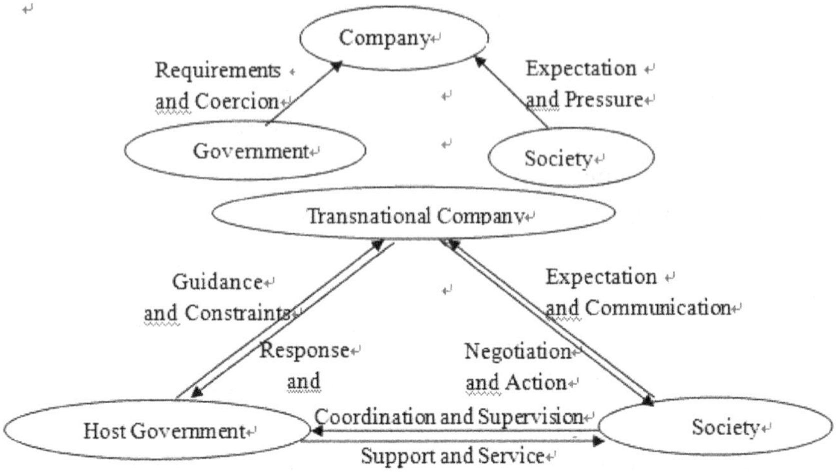

Figure 4-9 Transnational Corporate Social Responsibility from a Single Perspective and Dynamic Collaborative Perspective

However, they lack the right to speak, and their enthusiasm for fulfilling social responsibilities is not high. The essence of dynamic synergy is to regard the social responsibility of transnational corporations as a global social problem and achieve mutual benefit and harmony through the interaction and cooperation between transnational corporations, host governments and society. Without the efforts of transnational corporations, the social responsibility of transnational corporations will become an empty castle in the air. Without the supervision and guidance of the host government, the realization of the social responsibility of transnational enterprises lacks strong guarantee. Without the participation of society, it is impossible to create an atmosphere of public opinion to realize social responsibility and provide a flexible and diversified dialogue mechanism. A comparison of a single perspective with a dynamic collaborative perspective is shown in Figures 4-9.

4.4 Advantages of CSR Synergy Mechanism of Transnational Resource-oriented Enterprises

For the current situation of China and Mongolia, the social responsibility fostering mechanism of transnational resource-oriented enterprises should be based on the perspective of host countries, transnational resource enterprises and social synergy. The connotation of its manifestation is that, based on the promotion of the host country, the transnational resource-oriented enterprises actively fulfilling social responsibility as the main body, the overall supervision of the society as the basis, the basic model of legal regulation and media supervision as the guarantee. The three parties' collaborative perspective, multi-game, mutual checks and balances, internal and external considerations, market strategy, and gradual progress, in the process the entire mechanism is gradually matured to a comprehensive norm. The corporate social responsibility fostering mechanism, based on the host country, resource-oriented enterprises and social collaborative interaction perspective, is a mechanism model suitable for China and Mongolia. The elements, functions, paths, operating methods and strategies required for the CSR development mechanism are also fully in line with the current needs of cooperation between China and Mongolia. According to the current actual situation of China and Mongolia, it is difficult to solve the problem fundamentally by adopting any single perspective in the process of constructing a social responsibility fostering mechanism for transnational resource-oriented enterprises.

First of all, the host country cannot be regarded as the leader of the unilateral dependence of social responsibility as a transnational resource-oriented enterprise, because it is difficult for the host country to curb corporate infringement of social interests through its own compulsory. In fact, the host country and the enterprise are the interests of the community, precisely because in this way, the host country also needs the support of other parties. On the one hand, under the "Belt and Road" initiative, Mongolia's central task is to attract foreign investment and develop the economy. Transnational enterprises are the micro-carriers for foreign investment. The development of transnational enterprises is in sync with the development of Mongolia's economy. The relationship between a transnational corporation and a host government cannot be separated. However, the externalities of the company and the possible moral hazard are likely to harm the interests of society. On the other hand, the host government is the representative of the social interests, and has the obligation to safeguard the social interests through the state's coercive power, but this may affect the efficiency and economic development of transnational enterprises. The government in a dilemma is bound to repeatedly weigh.

In addition, it is not feasible to make social responsibility for society through the pressure of public opinion of the social group. Because the power of social groups is too small, there is no right to implement. At the present stage of the economic corridor between China and Mongolia, the degree of social interest outside the scope of national laws and government regulations and policies is very low. Although there are spontaneous social responsibility behaviors, the number of spontaneous social organizations is not only small, but most institutions are relatively loose, the quality of personnel is poor, funds are not sufficient, management level is low, and social influence is very limited. At the same time, most social organizations are greatly influenced by the government in terms of economy and behavior, and their independence is low. It is easy to become an appendage of the government, and it is difficult to realize the original intention and purpose of the organization. Therefore, the effect of urging them to undertake social responsibility of transnational corporations is not obvious. Relying on a single social force cannot fulfill social responsibility on a large scale.

For transnational enterprises, it is undoubtedly an idealized expectation that they should cultivate social responsibility as a kind of self-discipline. At present, both China and Mongolia lack the evolutionary conditions that CSR is driven by exogenous power to endogenous power. To achieve this transformation, it is necessary to provide a social environment of repeated game, solve the problem of social responsibility information asymmetry and establish an effective punishment and restraint mechanism. Some scholars have also suggested that it should be promoted by exogenous forces, and from the perspective of institutional structural changes, a dynamic mechanism for the balance of power structures of all stakeholders involved in multi-level participation and governance should be constructed.

The essence of the collaborative interaction perspective is to regard the social responsibility of transnational corporations as a global social problem, and achieve mutual benefit and harmony through the interaction and cooperation between transnational corporations, host governments and society. Without the efforts of transnational enterprises, CSR will become difficult to implement; without the supervision and guidance of the host government, the realization of corporate responsibility is not guaranteed; without the participation of society, it is impossible to create a public opinion atmosphere that provides social responsibility and provide flexible and diverse dialogue mechanism. The CSR fostering mechanism, based on the perspective of host government, transnational corporations and social synergy, is a mechanism model suitable for China and Mongolia.

1. It is conducive to giving full play to the role of the host government, transnational corporations and society

The government is the regulator of CSR. As the guardian of the public and the arbitrator who coordinates the private interests and social welfare of the enterprise, the host government establishes a sound and standardized legal and regulatory system through the state legislation and the exercise of public power, thus providing the procedural and institutionalized guarantee for the realization of CSR. The role of the government as a regulator is to promote the positive externalities of the firm, reducing or even eliminating negative externalities. To achieve the purpose of regulation, the government can combine economic control, social regulation, anti-unfair competition and monopoly control to control the social responsibility of enterprises that refuse social responsibility or exceed legal permission.

As the supervisor and promoter of social responsibility of transnational corporations, the social supervision and promotion means mainly through the guidance and regulation of the host government, such as non-governmental organizations, to carry out the necessary supervision and promotion of the status of social responsibility of transnational enterprises. For example, the typical means of supervision and promotion is to try to establish a social intermediary evaluation and review agency that is responsible for third-party certification between the government and the enterprise, which is responsible for the Non-governmental Organizations, and regularly provides relevant performance proof reports or evaluation results to stakeholders on a regular basis. At present, some areas of China are already exploring this aspect, and Mongolia has gradually paid more attention to this aspect.

As the implementers of social responsibility, transnational enterprises should cultivate their awareness of social responsibility, strengthen self-discipline spirit and behavior, and build the concept of taking the initiative to assume social responsibility. Many problems in the internal management of transnational corporations are not covered and concerned by current laws and regulations. The solution of these problems depends on the ethical level of enterprises and the awareness of social responsibility. By establishing corporate ethics such as the Code of Practice, transnational corporations can raise the ethical standards and consciously form an ethical bottom line between the government regulatory framework and the social supervision atmosphere, so as to minimize the pressure from the host government and society. This is the most important manifestation of the self-discipline spirit within the company and the fundamental internal cause of CSR. Therefore, the self-discipline spirit and behavior of transnational corporations play an irreplaceable role in the supervision system of CSR.

2. It reflects the governance ideas of seeking both temporary and permanent solutions

Transnational enterprises cultivate corporate social responsibility and formulate guiding policies and measures only for the link of corporate behavior. Although it is necessary, it is far from enough, because it solves problems only temporarily, not permanently. In many cases, companies may distort their behaviors because of profit-seeking motives and damage the social interests by taking CSR. Therefore, measures should also be taken from the motives of corporate behavior, to encourage enterprises to truly contribute to the host country, to the society, and take the initiative to assume social responsibility. This requires strengthening the social responsibility education for entrepreneurs. Compared with entrepreneurs in Western countries, Chinese entrepreneurs still have a large gap in their understanding of CSR. This gap is largely due to the education of entrepreneurs' social responsibility. Similarly, for Mongolia, facing the same problems as China, it is also necessary for enterprises to take the initiative to assume social responsibility from within. It is far from enough to rely solely on government or social supervision。

Based on the idea of seeking both temporary and permanent solutions, China and Mongolia should vigorously cultivate and develop NGOs. NGOs can establish flexible and diverse communication platforms and consultation mechanisms between enterprises and society, so that the contradiction between corporate interests and social interests can be resolved efficiently at the civilian level. With the continuous improvement of the legal system and the improvement of the democratic consciousness, the demands of self-management by spontaneous social organizations are increasing, which creates conditions for NGOs to play their roles. However, due to the influence of historical traditions, the influence of NGOs in the Chinese and Mongolian society has been very weak, and the space for exerting a role in solving social responsibility issues is still very limited. The influence of the government is very strong, almost touching every nerve ending of the social body. Therefore, the governments of China and Mongolia should support and encourage the development of NGOs, standardize and guide them to play their full role. To build a CSR fostering mechanism of government, enterprise and social synergy model, we should combine the mature experience of developed countries with the actual situation of China and Mongolia, and adopt the gradual evolution, through demonstration, maturity to comprehensive normative strategic principles. With the development of the CMEC, enterprises and society will develop simultaneously and mature together. Enterprises will gradually clarify the boundaries of responsibility and expand the scope of responsibility implementation. At the same time, more and more transnational enterprises will continue to improve their responsibilities, gradually change to normative, standard, uniform and international behaviors from strategic behavior.

3. It is conducive to the trade between China and Mongolia and maintaining friendly partnership

In recent years, China and Mongolia have witnessed rapid economic and trade development, and coal trade accounts for a large proportion of trade between the two countries (Zheng, 2013). Mongolia is a country with a strong focus on energy exports. China is the largest country for Mongolia's coal exports. China imports and transports coal from several major border trade cities in Inner Mongolia. This mutually beneficial economic and trade exchange has been continuously developing. Based on the context of the CMEC, resource-oriented enterprises fulfill their due social responsibilities in accordance with social needs, and obtain a good reputation and brand image, so that the partners of the enterprise can strengthen their trust in the enterprise and enable the resource-oriented enterprises to maintain good relations. This will strengthen the resource-trade cooperation between the two countries. China will undoubtedly remain to be Mongolia's largest trading partner and investor. The cooperation between the two countries has broad prospects. It is extremely important to vigorously develop bilateral trade between China and Mongolia.

Judging from the history of Sino-Mongolian trade development, both sides have experienced the process of choice-abandonment-reselection. It is currently the best period for trade cooperation between China and Mongolia. In this context, we should actively deepen the strategic cooperative partnership between China and Mongolia, optimize bilateral trade policies, expand trade cooperation, adjust industrial structure, improve China-Mongolia trade structure, and push China- Mongolia trade to a new level (Sun and Li, 2015).

4.5 The Possibility Study of CSR Synergy of Transnational Enterprises: Based on Dynamic Game Model

Game Theory is a behavioral tool for studying strategies, considering other people's predictive behavior and mutual independence of behavior. The core of Game Theory is that the action plans (strategies) implemented by the participating entities are interdependent. The outcome of the game after conflict or cooperation depends not only on the action plan adopted by the players, but also on the action decisions of other players. There are two basic assumptions about Game Theory: people are rational, that is, everyone will maximize their own interests under given constraints; people have conflicts in interactions, behaviors affect each other, and usually there is information asymmetry. In a Game model, the basic elements include: players, actions, information, strategies, payoffs, outcomes, and equilibrium etc.

Under the open policy of host country, transnational corporations entered the host country and had direct and close ties with the host country. On the one hand, transnational corporations play an active role in the economic and social development of the host country, not only promoting the investment and export expansion of the host country, industrial restructuring and upgrading, but also expanding the scale and operation range by introducing advanced technology and management experience. On the other hand, under the global profit maximization goal of transnational corporations, various conflicts between host countries and transnational corporations occur frequently. In addition, the lack of regulation of transnational corporations by host country regulations has adversely affected the economic development of the host country. In this way, the host country hopes that the transnational corporations will bear more social responsibilities and promote the coordinated development of the host country's economy and society. Transnational corporations are driven by profit maximization and always avoid or weaken their social responsibilities. The society has a scrutiny attitude towards the behavior of transnational corporations to fulfill their social responsibilities. Profit depends on the degree of social recognition. Only when the society agrees with the social responsibility behavior of transnational corporations, will transnational corporations benefit from it. All acts will not be subject to public opinion pressure from the host government and society. Ultimately, the ability of transnational corporations to actively fulfill their social responsibilities and performance is no longer unilaterally dependent on the behavior of one party, but the result of the game between the transnational corporation, the host government and the society.

4.5.1 Definition of Game Subject

1. Host government

The investment and management of transnational companies in the host country will have impact on many stakeholders other than shareholders. These stakeholders include employees, lenders, distributors, suppliers, as well as consumers, regulators, government agencies, the media, and local communities. Among these relevant stakeholders, the host government plays a leading role. It is not only the regulator of the behavior of transnational corporations, but also the maker of CSR standards and related policies in the host country. Therefore, the host government be an agent of other stakeholders as a gamer of confrontation with transnational corporations.

2. Transnational corporations

Transnational companies in the host country come from different countries and belong to different industries, and their scales are also different. Every transnational company has its own corporate culture and business model, and different countries have different standards for their management and supervision. Affected by this, different transnational companies are different in their treatment and handling of social responsibilities. If a specific transnational company is the main body of the game, it is difficult to grasp the degree and regularity of social responsibility in the host country, and it is very difficult to describe. In addition, it is impossible for the host country to develop different social responsibility standards and policies for transnational companies from different countries and sizes. In order to solve this problem, transnational corporations are understood as the collection of all transnational corporations in the host country and become the second game subject in the game.

3. Society

It mainly refers to other stakeholders, such as home countries, international organizations, NGOs, and media, which have an impact on the production and operation activities of enterprises other than enterprises and host countries. The advanced science and technology and management experience of transnational corporations has greatly promoted the global market economy. The cheap labor and resources of developing countries have brought benefits to transnational corporations. Driven by interests, some transnational corporations ignore the healthy living and living environment of the people and bring harm to society. When people realize that CSR will affect their own interests, the public will call on transnational corporations to assume their social responsibilities. Society is the third subject of the game.

4.5.2 Hypotheses and Analysis

Hypothesis 1

According to the stakeholder theory, this research divides the main body of CSR synergy into three: transnational enterprises, host governments and society. Therefore, the participants in the Game model are transnational corporations, host governments, and societies. It is assumed that the behaviors of transnational corporations, host governments, and social organizations are bounded and rational. Because the perceptual cognitive ability of the behavior subject is limited, the process of acquiring, storing, tracing and using the information of the behavior subject cannot be accurate, so the completely rational person does not exist. The goal of transnational corporations is to minimize the cost of fulfilling social responsibilities and maximize economic profits. The goal of the host government is to maximize economic benefits, as shown by tax and GDP growth. The intensity of social supervision on the social responsibility of transnational enterprises is relatively weak.

Hypothesis 2

Since transnational corporations are the main body of social responsibility, the host government and social actions generally decide the mode of action after considering the status of transnational corporations' responsibility, so the Game model is a Sequential Game. The order of the Game is as follows: First is transnational enterprise decision-making, choosing to actively fulfill social responsibility, or not fulfill social responsibility; Second, the host government and the society know the decision of the enterprise, then decide their own behavior, and agree (or disagree) with the behavior of the transnational enterprise to fulfill its social responsibility; Third, supervise and control the behavior of transnational corporations that fail to fulfill their social responsibilities, or let them go.

Hypothesis 3

Considering the complexity of the study, and the difficulty of quantifying the benefits, in this research, the values of the variables are represented by letters, and only their size is determined, which makes the model more appropriate and flexible. Suppose the profit of a transnational company is π, transnational companies can choose to fulfill their social responsibilities, or they can choose not to fulfill their social responsibilities. When a company fulfills its social responsibility, the enterprise needs to pay a certain cost, that is, the CSR cost (C); if the enterprise does not fulfill its social responsibility, the enterprise can use the cost of the current social responsibility for the next-stage production investment, and the increased income is γ (γ is its investment yield).

Hypothesis 4

For the behavior of transnational corporations to fulfill their social responsibilities, the host government and society can also have two choices: identifying corporate behavior; or disapproving corporate behavior. Assuming that the host government and the society recognize the behavior of CSR, the benefits that can be brought to the transnational enterprises are $r_1$and r_2, (r_1 and r_2 are greater than zero). At the same time, regardless of whether the host government and the society agree with the CSR, as long as the social economy can be a virtuous circle, the government and the society are all profitable, that is, the benefits of the host government and society are objectively existed. Assuming that the host government revenue is divided into λ R (R indicates the sum of the increased benefits of host governments and society due to the performance of social responsibilities by transnational corporations. λ is the proportion of the host government's revenue to the total revenue). Thus, the social benefit is $(1-\lambda)R$. As transnational corporations consciously fulfill their social responsibilities, it is assumed here that the cost of supervision of the host government and society for transnational corporations is zero.

Hypothesis 5

For the behavior of transnational corporations not fulfilling their social responsibilities, the host government and society may need to take certain measures to control and supervise, thus causing the reduction of the interests of transnational corporations, namely r_1 and r_2, representing the reduction of the interests of transnational corporations. At the same time, regardless of whether the host government and society regulate it, the tax revenue of the host government is generally relatively fixed, denoted by T. Assuming that the host government and society regulate simultaneously, their costs are respectively c_1 and c_2; if the host government controls and the society deregulates, then the control cost of host government is set as c_3 (obviously $c_3>c_1$). Currently, the cost of social regulation is zero. If the society strongly reacts to the failure of transnational corporations to perform social responsibility, and the host government does not control, the cost of social regulation will increase to c_3, that is, the social benefits will decrease c_3. Finally, if the host government and society do not control, their control costs are zero. The reduction of social benefits resulting from the non-fulfillment of social responsibilities by transnational enterprises is expressed in c_4. Since the host government's goal is tax and GDP growth, which is inversely proportional to the cost of social regulation, the host government tends to deregulate. At the same time, when the role of society is more obvious, the host government tends to deregulate, to obtain more gains. Thus the following relationship is derived, that is: $c_4>c_3>c_2>c_1$.

4.5.3 Construction of Three-party Dynamic Game Model

According to the above analysis, a Full Information Dynamic Game Model is used to construct a Three-way Dynamic Game Model, involving transnational corporations, host governments, and society, as shown in Figure 4-10.

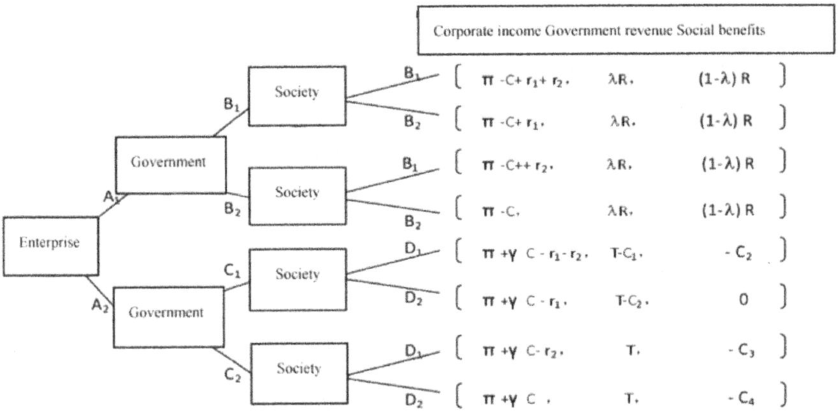

Figure 4-10 Transnational Corporation, Government and Social Expansion Game Model

As shown in Figure 4-10, based on the relationship between the three and their roles, the Game Diagram of transnational enterprise, host country government and social development is drawn, citing multiple letters to indicate the relationship and role, where A_1 and A_2 respectively represent the fulfillment and non-fulfillment of social responsibility by enterprises; B_1 and B_2 respectively represent the government and the society's recognition and disapproval for enterprises to fulfill their social responsibilities; C_1 and C_2 respectively indicate the action strategies adopted by local governments for enterprises not fulfilling social responsibilities: regulation and non-regulation; D_1 and D_2 indicate the actions or strategies taken by the society on enterprises' failure to fulfill their social responsibilities: supervision or non-supervision.

4.5.4 Equilibrium Analysis

In general, the Game Model can be divided into two situations, namely, transnational enterprises fulfill social responsibility and do not fulfill social responsibility.

1. The situation in which transnational corporations fulfill their social responsibilities

Whether or not host governments and societies agree with the performance of transnational corporations' social responsibilities, their interests exist objectively, respectively λ R and $(1-\lambda)$R. However, by analyzing the expectations of transnational corporations, society, and host governments under different circumstances, it can be found that only when the equilibrium path is $A_1B_1B_1$, that is, the transnational corporations fulfill their social responsibilities, and the host government and society agree that the enterprises fulfill their social responsibilities, transnational corporations have the greatest interests, and so do the interests of society as a whole (transnational corporations, host governments, and the sum of social interests). The investment of transnational corporations in social responsibility is highly correlated with the investment of society and host governments in transnational corporations. Raising the awareness of transnational corporations, society, and host governments to promote CSR is an important measure to promote the fulfillment of social responsibility of transnational corporations.

2. The situation in which transnational corporations fail to fulfill their social responsibilities

As far as transnational corporations are concerned, if the host government and society do not supervise transnational corporations to fulfill their social responsibilities, they will inevitably choose to fulfill their social responsibilities negatively, or even fail to fulfill their social responsibilities. For host governments, the pursuit of tax and GDP reverses the cost of government regulation. Therefore, the host government tends to loosen control over transnational corporations. At this time, the interests of the host government and enterprises have reached the maximum, but the social benefits are the smallest. Due to the status quo of "strong government and weak society", society can only choose not to supervise. Therefore, in the case of transnational corporations failing to fulfill their social responsibilities, the host government must choose not to control (C_2), and the society can only choose not to supervise (D_2). The final equilibrium result is $A_2C_2D_2$. Currently, the benefits of transnational corporations, host governments, and society are greater than in other situations. So, it is the only equilibrium of the Game. But in this situation, the social gain is the smallest, which is C_4, and the loss is the largest. This conclusion also explains why there is a significant lack of motivation to promote the fulfillment of CSR only from the inside of transnational enterprises, or to form the pressure or motivation mechanism between host government and society to promote the fulfillment of CSR.

The corporate social mechanism promoted by the three parties will ultimately realize the overall interests of the whole society, and the maximization of the individual interests of the transnational enterprises. Therefore, without prejudice to the interests of either party, only the three-way joint promotion mechanism is the path of maximizing revenue. Therefore, from the analysis of the Game Model, only when the host government and social supervision and transnational enterprises fulfill their social responsibilities, can the overall benefits of transnational enterprises, such as economic benefits, social benefits and environmental protection, be maximized. The Game analysis of this part lays the foundation for the construction of the social responsibility synergy mechanism of transnational enterprises.

4.6 CSR Synergy Mechanism Construction of Transnational Resource-oriented Enterprises in CMEC

4.6.1 Connotation of CSR Synergy Mechanism of Transnational Resource-oriented Enterprises

Based on the above analysis of the theoretical and practical basis of CSR synergy mechanism, this study defines the connotation of CSR synergy mechanism as follows:

CSR synergy mechanism is an enterprise social responsibility promotion model based on social contract theory, stakeholder theory and management coordination theory. It's a promotion model of CSR based on the rational allocation of resources, with transnational enterprises, host countries and social interaction and coordination. The basic connotation is: taking transnational corporations, host countries and social organizations as the mainstay; maximizing the integrated value of economy, society and environment as the driving force; creating potential by stimulating the value of transnational corporations and their stakeholders; and forming a comprehensive CSR promotion mode in which the three parties game, check and balance, interact and coordinate.

From the definition point of view, the connotation of the CSR synergy mechanism contains two basic contents, namely, synergy and mechanism. In terms of synergy, corresponding explanation has been given in the previous. Here we simply attribute it to a general term of a series of management thoughts, theories and methods formed by using the basic principles and methods of coordination to guide the progress of CSR. In this study, the CSR synergy mechanism is regarded as an interactive and collaborative system consisting of three subsystems: transnational corporation, host government and society. The mechanism refers to the form and movement principle of interaction, interconnection and mutual restraint between the three subsystems of transnational corporations, host governments and society, to maintain the good operation of the system, and the internal and essential working methods.

The main functions of the CSR synergy system mechanism are as follows:

1. Behavior-orientation role. Through the internal role of the CSR synergy mechanism, it guides and regulates the behavior of transnational corporations, host governments and society, promotes the implementation of CSR, and avoids the inefficiency of the three parties in promoting CSR.

2. Reduce costs and increase efficiency. The establishment of the CSR synergy mechanism is conducive to the communication and cooperation between transnational enterprises, host governments and society, reducing contradictions and conflicts, and thus achieving the goal of maximizing the comprehensive value of society.

3. Information transfer. The core of the operation of the CSR synergy mechanism lies in the rational allocation and utilization of resources, and information communication is the premise. The content of this part will be discussed in detail in the following.

4.6.2 Management and Economic Explanations of CSR Synergy Mechanism of Transnational Resource-oriented Enterprises

The research of CSR is an interdisciplinary study. In order to make clear the connotation and characteristics of CSR collaborative advancement, in this part, an explanation from the perspectives of management and economics will be given.

1. Management Explanation

Management is a science that systematically studies the basic laws and general methods of general organizational management activities. The basic principles, basic ideas and basic principles of management are the generalization and summary of various management disciplines and are the cornerstone of the entire management discipline system. In this part, the collaborative mechanism of CSR from the perspective of management characteristics will be explained.

First, management is targeted. Throughout the traditional CSR promotion mechanism, it is not difficult to find out whether it is in the field of economics or management, whether it is the strategic CSR proposed by Michael Porter or the "doing good to make money" proposed by Drucker (1984), or the relationship between the CSR and corporate financial performance, the basic starting point is the economic goals of the company, which are embodied in financial objectives, corporate competitiveness and corporate performance. Therefore, scholars try to persuade enterprises to consciously fulfill their social responsibilities from the perspective of theory and practice. The social responsibility behavior of enterprises is more manifested in the solution of specific social problems, and the satisfaction of the needs of specific social subjects, such as environmental protection, charitable donations, and employee welfare promotion etc. Here, CSR is a means, instead of a goal, and the social benefits brought about by it are more of the additional benefits that the company obtains when it realizes its own economic interests.

The CSR synergy model extends the financial value from the financial value to the comprehensive value of the economy, society and the environment, extending from the interests of shareholders to the value of stakeholders. It fully takes into account the social functions of enterprises and gives full play to the advantages of the roles, potentials, resources, etc. of various stakeholders. It is committed to the realization of comprehensive value, to coordinate the sustainable development of enterprise and society. Based on in-depth analysis of the relationship between people and enterprises, enterprises and enterprises, and enterprises and society in the process of business operations, it takes the maximization of social comprehensive value as the goal and motivation. Based on this, it works to reconstruct corporate mission, governance mechanism, development strategy, management system, operational process, promotion mechanism, social decision-making and function, government decision-making and function etc.

Second, Management activities are environmentally binding. Any organization exists in a certain internal and external environment and is bound by the environment. The production and operation activities of enterprises are usually affected by many factors, such as national policies, economic environment and laws. The purpose of the enterprise must exist outside the enterprise itself, and exist in the society (Drucker, 1973).

Stakeholder theory holds that the value of an enterprise cannot be directly created, and is obtained by creating value for stakeholders. The implementation path of CSR effect is from the internal to the external. The CSR behavior of the company to the stakeholders will first lead to the formation of external effects, such as investors' favor, employee satisfaction, customer praise and government support. Then, stakeholders are used as mediators to promote the internal effects of corporate profits, competitiveness, and growth, and to achieve economic consequences that affect the value of the company. These effects will prompt enterprises to consciously fulfill their social responsibilities.

Therefore, the purpose of the enterprise is no longer to maximize the interests of shareholders. The essence of the enterprise is the platform for the cooperation of stakeholders to create value. The stakeholders, including shareholders, pursue the diversified value of economic, social and environmental interests, and hope to achieve their respective pursuits through the platform of the enterprise. The main body of CSR promotion is no longer limited to a single enterprise, government or society. The stakeholders of the enterprise will play a role as the main body. This is essentially a model of CSR synergy with shared interests and shared responsibility.

Third, Management works through the effective use of the organization's resources to achieve organizational goals. Resources are the foundation of an organization's operations and a prerequisite for management. Different stakeholders have different relative resource advantages (such as information, resources, capabilities and willingness) in the process of pursuing different values (including economic, social and environmental values).

Only the CSR synergy mechanism can give play to the different advantages of each subject reasonably and create potential of value, after integrating the individual and the overall goal. It holds that each subject has rights and responsibilities depending on their level of contribution to value. Therefore, the CSR synergy mechanism is based on the common development of enterprises and various stakeholders. It deeply understands the diversity of social resources, and strives to stimulate and realize the potential, advantages and willingness of stakeholders to allocate various social resources, such as economy, society and environment. It focuses on the stage of social development (market and government maturity), national conditions and enterprise characteristics. It gives full play to the subjective initiative of stakeholders, strengthens cooperation, make up for market failure, government failure and social failure, and maximizes the optimal allocation of social resources, so as to realize the maximization of the comprehensive value of economy, society and environment of enterprise and social development.

In summary, the CSR synergy mechanism has achieved innovative development in terms of objectives, main body and implementation methods, compared with the various advancement mechanisms that existed before.

2. Economic explanation

Economics is a science that studies how to effectively allocate scarce resources to competing uses (Robbins, 1935). All economic problems stem from the contradiction between resource scarcity and infinite demand. Therefore, economics is the science of research choice. The scope of economics can be summarized as two major problems: first, the choice of what to produce, how to produce and for whom to produce; second, under what conditions the choice of personal interests can also enhance the interests of society.

First, let's come to the economic roots of CSR. In a certain period, the resources owned by enterprises are scarce. The essence of the operation process of enterprises is the process of configuring limited production materials according to the needs of different consumers, producing different quantities of products or providing different services. From the perspective of economics, the conflict and coordination between corporate profits and social responsibilities stem from the difference between corporate and social costs and benefits. When the enterprise and social costs and benefits are consistent, the market reaches a balanced state. When the two are inconsistent, for example in the tobacco, alcohol and other industries, when the cost of the enterprise is inconsistent with the social cost, the market will lose its intelligence. Market failures caused by differences in corporate and social costs and returns can lead to coordination problems of efficiency and equity. The CSR problem arises from the process of coordinating the contradiction between efficiency and fairness. Therefore, from the perspective of economics, CSR deals with the conflict between corporate profits and social goals from a social perspective, while the relationship between coordination efficiency and fairness is the economic root of CSR.

Second is the economic effect of CSR. No single subject exists in isolation. Every decision will have a certain impact on other topics. It is only based on the closeness of the relationship, and the degree and scope of its influence are different. This is the viewpoint advocated by the stakeholder theory. In connection with the current status of CSR implementation and the various social problems that arise, it is not difficult to see that corporate decision-making does not necessarily maximize social benefits, and even to some extent damage social interests. Therefore, what CSR synergy mechanism needs to solve is how to realize the unification of personal interests and social interests through resource allocation.

So far, we have extended the issue of CSR from the internal problems of the enterprise to an economic issue that deserves the attention and participation of the whole society. Therefore, the transformation of the CSR synergy mechanism is imperative. The CSR synergy grasps the promotion from a macro perspective. It promotes CSR through rational allocation of resources of enterprises and stakeholders and realizes the improvement of individual interests and overall interests.

4.6.3 Model Construction of CSR Synergy Mechanism of Transnational Resource-oriented Enterprise

1. Characteristics of CSR synergy

First, it is purposeful. The central goal of the CSR synergy is to produce a synergistic effect of "1+1+1>3". Collaborative promotion enables transnational corporations, host governments, and the society to cooperate with each other, which can reduce transaction costs and enable enterprises to fulfill their social responsibilities as the overall goal. The three parties work together to overcome (or significantly reduce) the series of negative effects (e. G., moral hazard under passive condition, active continuous operation risk) under non-cooperative states. It can mobilize the enthusiasm of the three parties, improve the complementary effects of relevant factors and the work efficiency of each subsystem in collaborative work, and achieve system function multiplication. The overall function of the system is a brand new overall effect of the combination of the functions of the subsystems. This combination can multiply the overall function of the system, and therefore far exceeds the sum of the functions of the subsystems. The purpose is obvious, that is, to make the result of the cooperation of the three parties greater than the sum of the result of the independent action of them.

Second, it has dominant trait. The synergy between the elements of CSR management system produces order parameters. The order parameter is a measure of the degree of order of the system, which dominates the system from disorder to order, and makes the system develop toward the desired goal, that is, solve social problems and create share value, and promote the sustainable development of society and enterprises. The order parameter is used as a mechanism to describe the orderly deepening of the self-organizing system, and as a parameter to describe the orderly evolution of the self-organizing system. Once it is generated through the interaction of elements, it will dominate the behavior of the elements. In summary, the order parameter must have the following three characteristics: one is the macroscopic parameter, which is the macroscopic overall behavior generated in the interaction of each subsystem. Second is the product of the collective movement of each subsystem, which is the representation and measurement of the cooperative effect. Third is the process in which it can control the behavior of various subsystems in the enterprise system and dominate the process of the overall evolution. Therefore, this research holds the idea that sustainability is the order parameter of the CSR management system.

Third, it has synchronization. The CSR synergy emphasizes that the coordination of numerous factors is synchronized in time and space. Synchronization in time requires that the synergistic elements should be closely connected and follows a common time reference; spatial synchronization requires coordinated coordination between the elements. Before the transnational enterprises, host governments and society have formed a synergy mechanism, the various subsystems exist independently, and there is no good correlation. When the interaction between the three parties forms a good social responsibility promotion mechanism, the synchronization will overcome the inconsistency between subsystems or elements and make the system in order. Each single element works simultaneously on the entire system, and finally achieves the goal.

Fourth, it has interactivity. The synergy effect among transnational enterprises, host government and society require cooperation and promotion among various factors, so as to enhance the effect of factors and achieve social responsibility, and the higher the interactivity between subsystems, the stronger the system as a whole, and the more stable the cycle of function-coupled causality. No matter what the conditions are, the three can maintain a stable synergy relationship, and the relationship between each other will not change, which will be maintained in real time. If the system has been coupled successfully, the system activity will be interrupted if it is disconnected. If the link is weak, it will become a bottleneck, which will affect the overall function and effect. To maintain the coordination and stability between the three, the interaction between them have to be strengthened, and anyone of them cannot leave the general system, make would make the synergy weakened.

Fifth, it has mutually beneficial attributes.

While the entire mechanism works, each factor is paying its own strength, and each of the associated stakeholders gets a benefit that is greater than the cost, so it is beneficial to either of the elements provided on the entire system. The interests of one party are not satisfied to the detriment of the interests of the other two. Whether it is the transnational enterprise itself, a host government or a society, it will gain greater benefits while transnational corporations assume social responsibilities, so the whole system has mutually beneficial attributes.

2. Conceptual model of CSR synergy mechanism

Social responsibility collaborative management system is a compound system, $S=\{S_1, S_2, \cdots S_k\}$ (4.1), associated by subsystems at all levels. For the convenience of discussion, this study only considers the primary subsystem of the system $S_i (i=1,2,3)$ (transnational corporations, host governments, society). So, the composite approach of the system can be further abstracted as: $s=f(s_1, s_2, s_3)$, where f is called the compound factor.

The essence of the CSR synergy is: based on the structural and functional characteristics of the CSR management system, find an effective promotion mechanism, so that under the action of m, according to the specific evaluation criteria, make the overall function of the system E(S) greater than the sum of the effects of the three subsystems, and take the maximum, namely:

$$\max\left\{E^m(s)-\sum_{i=1}^{3}E^f(s_i)\right\}, q\in Q_0, m(q)\in Q_1, m\in M \quad (4.2)$$

In the equation, "q" is the order parameter of the system; Q_0 and Q_1 are the initial state conditions and evolution constraints of the system. "m" is the propulsion mechanism of S, and the set of "m" is denoted as M, which is the synergy mechanism of CSR management.

3. Model framework of CSR synergy mechanism

Further, to better explain the systemic and synergistic realization process of the CSR synergy mechanism. Based on the previous research, the whole theory is integrated, and finally the stakeholder theory and management synergy are presented in this study. Combined with the current development of China and Mongolia, the status quo of CSR promotion in the context of CMEC, the CSR synergy mechanism model is constructed, as shown in Figure 4-11.

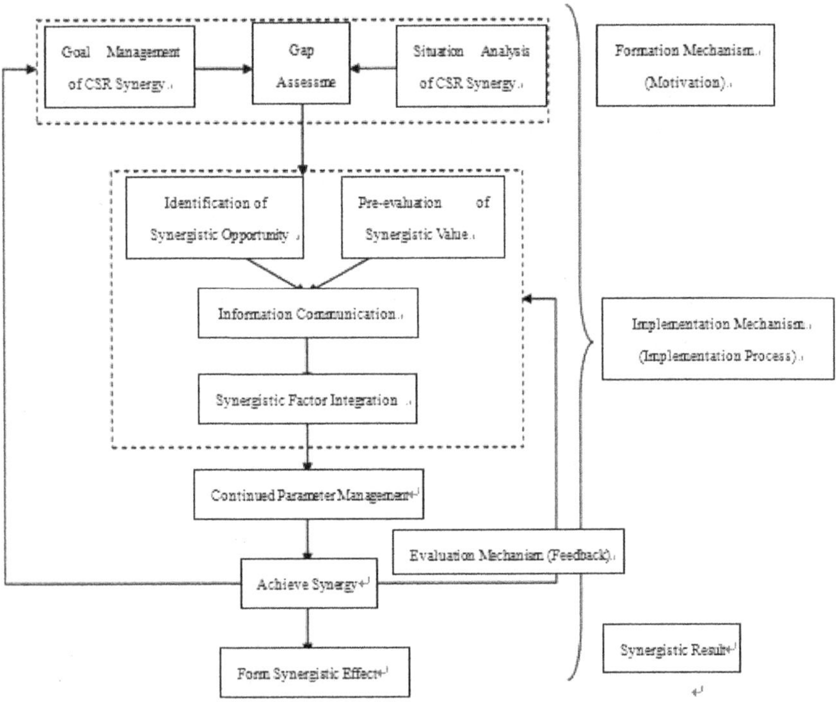

Figure 4-11 Model of CSR Synergy Mechanism for Transnational Corporations

The CSR synergy mechanism model can be decomposed into three major mechanisms: synergy formation mechanism, collaborative realization mechanism and evaluation mechanism. The formation and integration of the three mechanisms ensure that the mechanism is a self-operating system, which is composed of transnational enterprises and host governments. It consists of three subsystems, which interact, connect and restrict each other.

(1) Synergistic formation mechanism

According to the idea of synergy, the essence of synergy lays is that through the cooperation and coordination of subsystems or sub-elements within the system, it ensures that the three can be effectively connected and thus form an orderly system process. The mechanism of synergy formation is to explain why synergy can be achieved, which is the starting point and premise of the synergy mechanism. Specifically, the synergy formation mechanism includes three parts: collaborative promotion of goal management, status assessment and gap analysis. These three components can ensure that the synergy formation mechanism is more complete and can play a real-time monitoring role for the entire formation process. The final goal can be achieved through assessment of the status quo and gap analysis.

The CSR synergy of transnational resource-oriented enterprises in CMEC aims at realizing the optimization of social responsibility (economic responsibility, legal responsibility and moral responsibility) of the enterprises (balance of stakeholders), and developing the economic, social and ecological benefits in a dynamic balance. The system takes sustainable development as a parameter, integrates transnational resource-oriented enterprises, host governments, and social orderly development to achieve synergy.

In the process of the CSR synergy, transnational corporations, host governments, and social entities have achieved process coordination, organizational coordination, information coordination, and resource coordination. All social responsibility decision-making actions can be consistent throughout the process. They keep a close connection, share the information and resources, to achieve the goal of three major entities coexisting with each other. Moreover, as a main body of internal promotion, transnational resource-oriented enterprises need to strengthen the response mechanism and self-discipline mechanism at the level of economic, legal and moral responsibility. Starting from itself, it makes their behavior comply with the legal and economic constraints, ensures that the host country under the call of the government, strengthens communication mechanism in the level of moral responsibility, makes use of CSR behavior to drive other transnational companies to follow, forms a huge influence in the whole industry chain, and urges the whole industry to absorb the social responsibility of the economic effect.

In terms of external promotion, at the economic level, the host government and society form a pressure mechanism and incentive mechanism. Under the policy pressure of the host government, transnational enterprises respond to the decisions of the host government through decision-making behavior. For the society, the social responsibility behavior of transnational corporations will bring long-term sustainable economic benefits, and the society will bring unlimited development power to transnational corporations. At the legal level, host governments and society establish normative mechanisms and supervision mechanisms, and the government establishes rules and regulations through its compulsory system, while the public exercises its supervisory role. At the moral level, introduce evaluation, guidance and dissemination mechanisms, including the paradox of transnational corporations, host governments and societies on CSR behaviors, evaluate the behavior of transnational corporations, and guide and disseminate corporate behavior, no matter how transnational corporations, society and the host government have a close interaction in the synergy mechanism.

(2) Synergy implementation mechanism

There is still a long way to go between the formation of ideas and the realization of synergies. The synergistic realization mechanism is the core of the synergy. The synergy mechanism is based on the formation mechanism, which mainly includes the identification of collaborative opportunities, the pre-evaluation of the synergy value of elements, information communication, and integration of synergistic elements. The entire implementation mechanism is mainly achieved through effective cooperation between the various elements. Mutual information communication, resource allocation and personnel support are indispensable. In the context of the entire CMEC, only the effective combination of information, resources, personnel and other elements can ensure the realization of the whole synergy mechanism.

The opportunity identification of synergy mechanism emphasizes that transnational resource-oriented enterprises, host governments, and societies discover and mine synergistic factors to determine when and where there is synergy. Synergy opportunities are often generated when the system is in a phase of change or "critical point", and follows the following principles: First, the principle of adaptability, in harmony with the external environment: Second, the principle of complementarities, seeking complementary resources within and outside the subsystem, taking advantage of each other's strengths to form an overall advantage and enhance competitiveness; Third, the principle of mutual benefit and mutual trust, transnational corporations, host governments, and society build a community of interests, and build mutual trust, which are conducive to rapid response to risks; Fourth, the principle of minimizing costs, assessing synergy costs to judge feasibility .

The value budget of synergy mechanism has a valuable feedback effect on opportunity identification and affects synergy factors. The value budget evaluates the synergy opportunities by assessing the actual value generated by the interaction of synergistic factors, that is, the value generated by the synergy minus the cost brought by the synergy. The positive value is a reasonable synergy. In the same way as seeking the maximum value of synergistic efficiency, it selects the synergistic factor that brings the actual value as the maximum value. In practice, it is difficult to measure the actual value accurately.

Through opportunity identification and value budgeting, favorable synergistic factors have been screened out. The integration of elements and the generation of order parameters is exactly the effective process of CSR promotion. The integration of synergy elements is a coordinated way of integration, interaction and necessary reorganization of elements, so that different synergistic elements can be merged into a harmonious organic whole to achieve the overall effect. The integration of elements of transnational corporations, host governments, and society is characterized by consistency, systemicity, asymptoticity, and mutual benefit. Gradually, under the unstable state, the order parameters that govern the development of the system, sustainable development, is developed. Transnational enterprises adjust their business strategies, the host governments change their functions, and the society takes an active part in forming an orderly system, in which way an orderly system can be formed.

The result feedback is to compare the synergistic effect with the goal, to examine the synergy effect, and then continue to operate or modify the system to form a benign continuous cycle.

(3) Synergy evaluation mechanism

In theory, through the operation of the synergy formation mechanism and the synergy realization mechanism, the CSR synergy system moves from disordered state to orderly state, and finally can achieve synergy effect, resulting in a synergistic result, that is, maximize the comprehensive value of society while achieving the goals of each subject. However, whether this synergistic effect is the effect achieved by the synergy mechanism, and whether it is the optimal result achieved in the whole, it must be measured according to certain standards. At this time, the formation of a synergy mechanism can compare the output of the system with the target. If there is a big gap between the result and the target, it means that there is a problem in one or some links in the process of synergy, and the relevant stakeholders modify the whole mechanism through some effective actions, aiming at narrowing the gap between results and expectations. The synergy evaluation system is not only used to evaluate the results, but also a guiding framework for measures to implement synergistic mechanisms.

Chapter 5

CSR Synergy Implementation of Transnational Resource-oriented Enterprises in CMEC

In the last chapter, the conceptual model of the CSR synergy mechanism of transnational resource-oriented enterprises is constructed. The model can be decomposed into three major mechanisms: synergy formation mechanism, synergy realization mechanism and synergy evaluation mechanism. This chapter will elaborate and explain on the three mechanisms, and further expound the specific implementation process of the synergy mechanism.

5.1 CSR Synergy Formation Mechanism of Transnational Resource-oriented Enterprises in CMEC

The CSR formation mechanism of transnational resource-oriented enterprises is not a simple unity, nor will it be formed naturally. Instead, the main bodies are guided by the concept of CSR synergy based on fully understanding their own responsibilities and conditions. It is a purposeful, reasonably organized course of action, designed to explain why CSR is promoted through a synergy mechanism. This part explores the relationship between the overall goal and the specific goals of CSR synergy, the current situation of CSR promotion, and the analysis of the gap between goals and reality. It seeks solutions to shorten the gap, and then explain the formation mechanism of the CSR synergy mechanism.

5.1.1 CSR Synergy Goal Management of Transnational Resource-oriented Enterprises

The CSR synergy mechanism of transnational resource-oriented enterprises is a horizontal synergy. It is a collaborative behavior of multiple individuals (transnational resource-oriented enterprises, host governments, and societies). Therefore, goal management involves the management of overall goals and individual goals. The significance of goal management is to ensure the consistency of each subsystem's goals with the overall goals.

The CSR synergy mechanism of transnational resource-oriented enterprises aims at maximizing the comprehensive value of society. It is to achieve economic, legal, environmental protection and moral goals and other conditions to improve the overall social benefits. Obviously, the four specific goals of this mechanism are the specific content of CSR (based on Karl's four-level theory of CSR). Therefore, the overall goal of the CSR synergy mechanism is the integration of four specific goals.

The three main bodies that promote the CSR synergy of transnational resource-oriented enterprises are: transnational resource-oriented enterprises, host governments, and society. Their goals are different. Transnational resource-oriented enterprises are fundamentally profit-seeking. The host governments and society are committed to the normal operation of the domestic market, environmental protection, and the harmonious development of society. Therefore, to a certain extent, the objectives of each subject coincide with the content of CSR. However, the realization of these goals cannot be treated in isolation. Moreover, the goal of the synergy CSR mechanism of transnational resource-oriented enterprises cannot be considered as the simple addition of specific goals. In the process of realizing the CSR synergy mechanism of transnational resource-oriented enterprises, it is necessary to internalize the synergy goal of maximizing social comprehensive value into each subject and cooperate with the strength of each subject to achieve the overall goal. The relationship between them is shown in Figure 5-1.

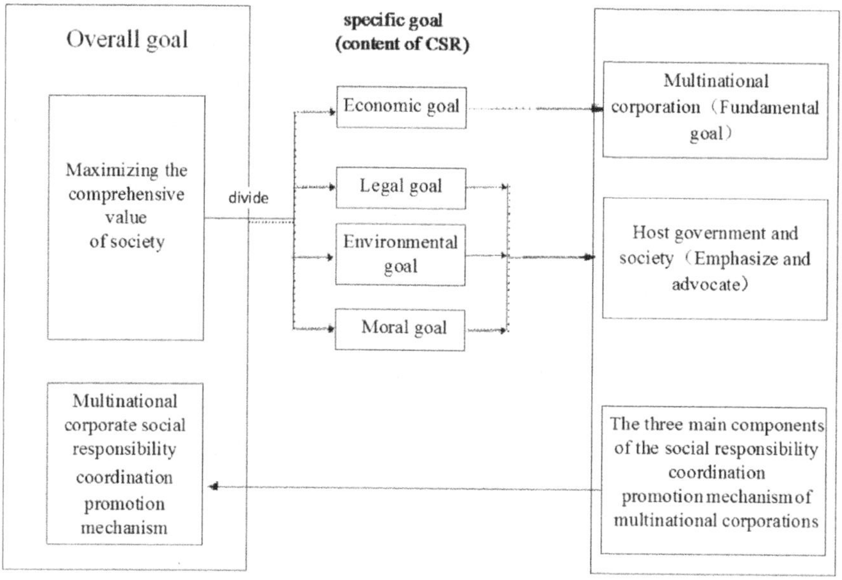

Figure 5-1 Target Management System for CSR Synergy Mechanism of Transnational Resource-oriented Enterprises

Therefore, in the CSR synergy mechanism of transnational resource-oriented enterprises, there is consistency between the overall goal and the subsystem goal. No matter how much difference between the overall goal and the individual goal, the deep content or essence they point to is the same. Both are in pursuit of the effect of the overall function, and to obtain the maximum value. The realization of the comprehensive value maximization depends on the realization of the objectives of each subsystem, and the improvement of the overall social benefit can create a good environment for each subsystem to achieve its goals.

5.1.2 CSR Status Assessment Indicator Model of Transnational Resource-oriented Enterprises

To achieve the system's collaboration, it is necessary to evaluate the current situation of promoting the social responsibility of transnational enterprises and recognize the gap between reality and ideal. The content of the status assessment can be divided into two aspects, namely, the assessment of the status quo of the transnational resource-oriented enterprises themselves to promote CSR, and the assessment of the status quo of the host government and the society to promote CSR. This study adopts the literature research method and based on the full consideration of the current actual situation, it establishes the evaluation model of the status quo of CSR. The model establishes four basic indicators for evaluation, respectively CSR awareness of transnational enterprises (U1), CSR promotion institutional construction of transnational enterprises (U2), CSR promotion resource guarantee of transnational enterprises (U3), and CSR promotion ability evaluation of transnational enterprises (U4). To explain the specific content of the four indicators, the four indicators are operationally defined in Table 5-1.

Table 5-1 Evaluation Model of the Status Quo of CSR Promotion in Transnational Enterprises

	Operational Definition of Indicators		
Evaluation Index	**Transnational Enterprises**	**Host Governments**	**Society**
U_1 CSR awareness	Do transnational corporations have a sense of compliance and compliance, establish a sense of consciously fulfilling their social responsibilities, and establish a sense of stakeholder awareness?	Whether to pay attention to the promotion of CSR, whether to establish awareness of promoting CSR, whether to focus on CSR promotion and education and to focus on the concept and awareness of CSR?	Whether to pay attention to the promotion of CSR, whether to establish awareness of promoting CSR, whether to focus on CSR promotion and education and to focus on the concept and awareness of CSR?
U_2 CSR institutional construction	Do transnational enterprises establish a CSR information disclosure mechanism, whether to establish a CSR	Is there a special law to promote CSR and continuous improvement, whether to establish a CSR indicator system,	Whether to establish a CSR indicator system, whether to establish corresponding industry standards,

	Operational Definition of Indicators		
Evaluation Index	**Transnational Enterprises**	**Host Governments**	**Society**
	indicator system, whether to establish a CSR assessment system, and whether to establish a department specializing in CSR?	whether to set up a department to promote CSR and to supervise the performance of transnational companies by means of administration, auditing and certification?	and whether to establish a department dedicated to promoting CSR?
U_3 **CSR resource guarantee**	Whether to provide special funds to support the implementation of CSR, whether to provide other material resources to support employees to fulfill their social responsibilities, and whether to deploy specialized personnel for CSR promotion?	Are there special funds and other material resources for supporting transnational companies, host governments, and society to implement or promote CSR, such as material support, human support, knowledge support, policy support, information support, etc., whether there are specialized personnel engaged in CSR work, whether to provide resources for the study of transnational CSR, whether to reward transnational companies with good performance, such as government procurement behavior or direct economic incentives?	Are there special funds and other material resources for transnational companies to fulfill their social responsibilities or promote CSR support, such as material support, human support, knowledge support, policy support, etc., whether there are specialized personnel engaged in CSR work?
U_4 **CSR ability evaluation**	Whether to conduct CSR training for employees and successfully organize large-scale CSR activities or conferences?	What is the status of CSR law enforcement capabilities, the ability to organize large-scale CSR activities or meetings, and the ability to advance in international CSR?	Evaluation of the strength and influence of CSR supervision

Three points about the evaluation indicator model:

First is the source of the indicator. Using China National Knowledge Internet (CNKI) as the source of data literature, and the "Corporate Social Responsibility Implementation" and "Corporate Social Responsibility Promotion" as keywords, to search the journals of SCI, EI, CSSCI and conference reports for 2016 and 2017, there were 1,681 periodicals in the period and 27 conference reports. After careful reading and screening, 100 periodicals and 15 conference reports were intensively read and organized. Combined with the status of China's CSR promotion, the evaluation indicators are identified as four evaluation indicators, and these four indicators are operationally defined according to research questions and research results.

Second, the indicator model is based on a single perspective analysis, mainly for the independent behavioral performance of current enterprises, governments and society in promoting CSR. Due to the differences between enterprises, governments and society, we have separately defined these four indicators, highlighting the functionality of different actors. As the direct main body of CSR promotion, enterprises mainly examine their self-consciousness and behavioral performance in the promotion of CSR. The government and society act as external driving force, mainly investigate their influence on CSR, and the guarantees and support provided to motivate companies to fulfill their social responsibilities.

5.2 CSR Synergy Implementation Mechanism of Transnational Resource-oriented Enterprises in CMEC

The synergistic formation mechanism only explains the feasibility or motivation of synergy in the conceptual form or theoretical sense. To realize this feasibility into reality, it is necessary to study the realization mechanism of synergy. Therefore, the mechanism of synergy formation mainly solves the problem of coordination, and the synergy implementation mechanism solves the problem of how or how to coordinate. In this part, it will explain the synergy implementation mechanism through the research on synergy opportunity identification, pre-evaluation of synergistic value, information communication, factor integration, and order parameter management.

5.2.1 Identification Synergistic Opportunity

Identifying synergistic opportunities is a breakthrough in implementing management collaboration, mainly to find out how to seek synergy opportunities in the implementation process, that is, to find out where the system may create synergies. Only by accurately and timely identifying the opportunities for synergy, can the various management measures and methods around the synergy opportunities be obtained to achieve the effect of management coordination. At the same time, the identification of collaborative opportunities is also the basis for managing collaborative follow-up behavior. It is believed in this study that there are two opportunities for the CSR synergy of transnational resource-oriented enterprises:

One is the concept of Win-Win. To achieve economic benefits for transnational corporations, the host government and society hope that transnational corporations will fulfill their obligations to protect the environment, protect the legitimate rights and interests of employees, and make due contributions to the development of the host country. Enterprises in China and Mongolia do an excellent job in the field CSR. On the one hand, it helps maintain the stability of the Sino-Mongolian border, and on the other hand, it can promote the economic development of China and Mongolia. The economic benefits of transnational corporations are of course important, but if transnational corporations neglect social responsibilities, on the one hand, it will cause instability in the border areas of China and Mongolia, on the other hand, it will affect the economic interests of enterprises, and thus affect the sustainable development of China-Mongolia economic corridor.

The host government has always acted as the main body of CSR and played a role in supervision and regulation. But when the host government's coercion makes the transnational corporations conflict with the interests of the society, the host government only hopes that the transnational corporations will sacrifice their own interests, which will lead to inefficient performance of transnational corporations. From a social point of view, the public, news media, and non-governmental international organizations are very concerned about the fulfillment of social responsibility of transnational corporations and strive to propose an evaluation mechanism for social responsibility of transnational corporations, trying to influence the fulfillment of social responsibility of transnational corporations through their own activities. However, society is not the subject of CSR and in some respects does not have the conditions and technology to fulfill social responsibility.

Due to the lack of effective communication and cooperation between the three, the current transnational corporations have inferior performance, and the influence of the host government and society is limited. However, after a long-term game between transnational corporations, host governments and society, it can finally achieve a win-win situation, that is, through the establishment of a model of transnational corporations, host governments, and social tripartite cooperation, to form an orderly system to jointly promote social responsibility, to maximize social benefits while achieving their respective value requirements.

Second, the advantages complement each other. The three main bodies of the CSR synergy of transnational corporations have their own characteristics and advantages. Transnational enterprises can embody the fulfillment of social responsibility in all aspects of production and operation by establishing social responsibility awareness, arranging special funds, and arranging personnel specializing in CSR. Moreover, in terms of the implementation of social responsibility of transnational corporations, the advantages of technology, resources and manpower of transnational corporations are more prominent. Therefore, the initiative of transnational corporations is crucial. In the process of promoting social responsibility, the host government, through legislation and law enforcement, punishes transnational corporations that do not fulfill their social responsibilities, encourages corporate social responsibility to perform better transnational corporations, establishes a transnational corporate social responsibility evaluation system, and so on, to create a good environment for transnational corporations to fulfill social responsibilities. The authority of the host government also provides an important guarantee for the promotion of social responsibility of transnational corporations.

The host government plays an important role in shaping the environment and providing a fair mechanism. Social organizations have gradually shown their role in the promotion of social responsibility of transnational corporations, especially the extensive influence of the media. On the one hand, it is the tool for communication between host governments and transnational corporations; on the other hand, through its own influence, it can exert certain pressure on the fulfillment of the social responsibility of transnational corporations to promote the responsibility of transnational corporations. Based on the above analysis, if transnational corporations, host governments, and societies can achieve cooperation and complement each other's advantages, considerable progress will be made. In the CMEC, Mongolia has enough resources, lack of funds, but lack of technology; while China has funds, technology, and market, which forms industry complement with Mongolia. Only by better fulfilling CSR can transnational corporations achieve sustainable development of the CMEC, bring more benefits to transnational corporations, and achieve a win-win situation for both countries.

5.2.2 Pre-evaluation of Synergistic Value

Pre-evaluation of synergistic value refers to the pre-evaluation of the value or contribution of the synergy of factors in the collaborative process based on identifying synergistic opportunities. This is the key to the formation of synergy mechanism. Its leading role is reflected in two aspects: First, by pre-evaluating the synergistic value of the elements in the collaborative process, it is possible to compare the synergistic cost and the synergistic value generated in the collaborative process, and then determines how much the factor synergy contributes to the entire collaborative process. Second, through the pre-evaluation of the synergistic value of factors, the value embodied in the synergistic process can be determined in advance, which is conducive to the rational and fair distribution of synergistic factors. The benefits brought by the synergistic effect can ensure the smooth progress of the subsequent synergistic behavior. Considering the conclusion of the game described above and the effect created by the cooperative mechanism of social responsibility of transnational enterprises, this study believes that the synergistic value is mainly reflected in the following aspects:

First, realize the residual value of cooperation. The residual value of cooperation refers to the added value of other stakeholders' values brought by each entity while achieving the value pursued by it. According to the above content of social responsibility of transnational corporations, namely economic responsibility, legal responsibility, environmental protection responsibility, moral responsibility and charity responsibility, from the perspective of transnational enterprise itself, whether it is to maintain the reputation of transnational enterprises, or to enhance the competitiveness of enterprises, the fundamental purpose for the transnational corporations to complement CSR is to achieve economic interests, and environmental protection, employee rights protection, and even the improvement of the overall social benefits can be regarded as the added value of the responsibility of transnational enterprises, namely the residual value. If effective synergy can be achieved, each entity can achieve its own goals while promoting the realization of stakeholder interests, thereby improving overall efficiency.

Second, realize the value of idle resources and create potential. The scarcity of resources is the source of all social problems. Although resources can flow between departments under the conditions of free competition and are configured through the invisible hand of the market, the resource allocation of each department is not balanced. In a certain period of time, some departments have relatively few resources, while some others have surplus resources. At this time, social resources are not made the best use. If these resources are fully used, more value will be generated. For example, if a transnational resource-oriented enterprise develops a very energy-efficient production process and wants to improve its production equipment, but because of the immature technology and lack of funds, the cost of equipment is relatively high. At this point, the company has two choices: on the one side, in order to save energy, protect the environment, reduce their own profits, it puts the equipment into production, and it is conceivable that the company's income will not be ideal for a long time; on the other side, for the sake of short-term interests, the enterprise abandon the production equipment and continue to produce in a high-energy consumption way.

Such a choice is the result of the company's own treatment, but if the host government and society are taken into consideration, the results will be very different. If the transnational corporations communicate effectively with the host government and the fund organization, to let the host government and society understand the prospects for sustainable development of the equipment, the host government or the fund organization has some idle funds, which can directly subsidize the losses of the enterprise, and help companies improve their technology, or the government subsidizes consumers. Through this way of cooperation, the reasonable utilization of surplus resources is realized, and potential value is created. Therefore, the CSR synergy mechanism of transnational enterprises can achieve the purpose of rational allocation of resources through the flow of resources, and thus create more social value.

5.2.3 Information Communication

Information communication refers to all communication methods adopted to enable the subsystems in the system to better generate synergies and make the system function. Information communication is the basis of the synergy mechanism. The core to realize the CSR synergy mechanism of transnational enterprises is the integration and allocation of resources. The biggest problem it faces is information isolation. If there is no communication, there is no coordination, and it is impossible to achieve the overall goal of the system. Synergistic opportunity identification and synergistic value pre-assessment can only be clearly understood, recognized and accepted by system members based on extensive and in-depth communication and communication within and outside the transnational enterprise system. Only when it is transformed into a member's conscious behavior, can it give full play to its due value and ensure the smooth implementation of synergy. Information runs through the entire system, and information communication is mainly to achieve the following work:

First, increase trust and reach a consensus on cooperation through communication. Although in theory, transnational corporations, host governments, and societies have the goal of coherence in promoting social responsibility, and have a sense of cooperation, if there is no communication, a true consensus of cooperation cannot be reached.

Second, reduce information asymmetry and the cost of decision and action. One of the premises of decision-making is the grasp of information. The more information is mastered, the higher the accuracy of decision-making. Through communication, information asymmetry between transnational corporations, turbulent governments and society can be reduced. For transnational companies, the influence of the external environment is very crucial. When making decisions, companies must measure their own resource capabilities, and consider the external environment, especially the host government's policies and social mainstream values. All of these require effective communication of information. The host government exists as a service organization, and its policies are formulated according to the needs of the development of various social entities. Therefore, the host government needs to obtain relevant decision-making information. In the process of information dissemination and communication, the media and the network play a significant role, and are the bridge of information communication.

Third, communicate resource information and allocate resources reasonably. Transnational corporations, host governments, and society do not always advertise their own resource usage and storage status. Only through communication can they be known. Therefore, communication is the basis for resource allocation and effective circulation.

5.2.4 Synergistic factor integration

Synergistic factor integration is a process of system ordering, and it is also a process of balancing, selecting and synergizing synergistic factors based on synergistic opportunity identification, factor synergy value pre-evaluation and communication. The purpose of factor integration is to maximize the advantages of each subsystem, make up for the deficiencies, and make the synergistic system produce the overall functional effects through complementary advantages. Its role is to improve or break through the bottlenecks and constraints that limit the development of synergy systems, so that synergistic factors play the best role to achieve the related value-added activities and the overall functional effects of the system. Michael Porter believes that the integration is a strategy, not just a series of activities, and the real strategy is a series of interactive activities. Jieming Rui believes that the integration is the process of integrating and coordinating the activities of individuals and departments in the organization (Rui, 1999).

1. Principles to be followed in the synergistic factor integration

First is the principle of trust. If there is no trust, it is difficult to establish the CSR synergy mechanism of transnational enterprises. If there is no trust, then the three parties of cooperation will fall into the non-cooperative dilemma. The establishment of the principle of trust first requires partners to respect laws and regulations and respect the bottom line of value. Secondly, it is possible to reach a consensus on common responsibility. Only when transnational corporations, host governments, and societies can reach a consensus on maximizing the value of society's comprehensive value, will it be possible to form a cooperative alliance of shared interests and responsibilities, and then make efforts to achieve economic goals, environmental protection goals, and social goals.

Second is the principle of complementarity. The principle of complementarity is the first principle of synergy. It refers to the free flow of resources between the various entities in the process of forming a synergistic system. Each subject can use their own resources and can also use the resources of other subjects. The purpose is to achieve optimal allocation of resources and maximize the value of resource use to maximize overall benefits. In the CSR synergy mechanism of transnational enterprises, complementary resources are mainly concentrated in human, financial, material, technical and information resources. Through the collaborative integration of elements, it can bring benefits to transnational corporations and their stakeholders. This is the driving force for transnational corporations, host governments and society to follow the synergy.

Third is the principle of effective motivation. The CSR implementation of transnational corporations will incur a certain cost. Although communication can reach a consensus of collaboration, effective incentives are needed, to ensure that transnational corporations and their stakeholders can carry out in-depth and comprehensive cooperation on the basis of trust. There are two kinds of effective motivation, respectively internal motivation and external motivation.

Internal motivation includes two aspects: First, in the transnational enterprises, through the cultivation of corporate employees' sense of social responsibility awareness, establish a sense of consciously fulfilling social responsibility, and improve the ability of transnational corporations to perform their duties; Second, actively advocate the goal of maximizing comprehensive value, encourage the participation of stakeholders, and create a cooperative culture, self-discipline culture, win-win culture and innovation culture for the extensive cooperation of transnational corporations, host governments and society, establish smooth communication channels, and provide the necessary resources to support the cooperation with stakeholders.

External motivation focuses on the role of the host government and society in the CSR complementation process of transnational corporations. They require stakeholders to actively display and communicate their superiority and disadvantages, share knowledge, information and resources that create specific value with the enterprise, and adopt specific implementation measures based on the cooperation mechanism of factor synergy. Specific external motivations include legal or social norms motivations, ideological motivations and knowledge tools motivations. Legal or social norms motivations refer to social norms such as certain laws and regulations and industry conventions or social value advocacy, requiring transnational corporations to promote the realization of social and environmental values while pursuing basic economic goals. Ideological motivations mean that transnational enterprises make rational decisions through the host government and social construction, so that they can consciously realize and be willing to pursue the maximization of the comprehensive value of economy, society and environment. Knowledge tools motivations refer to that by providing specific innovative knowledge and cooperation tools for transnational enterprises and their stakeholders, to encourage transnational enterprises and stakeholders to give full play to their initiative and creativity, and consciously serve to maximize the comprehensive economic, social and environmental value.

2. The content of synergistic factor integration

The factor integration of CSR synergy mechanism of transnational resource-oriented enterprises is mainly the integration of resource factors. The resource refers to the general term for the internal and external resources (including the relationship between resource factors) and the capability factors that can be controlled and influenced by each entity and can be used to promote the fulfillment of CSR. The investment in CSR is a long-term investment, and various resources are the material basis for the fulfillment of CSR. From a morphological point of view, resources include tangible resources and intangible resources. Tangible resources including such as direct investment etc. Intangible resources including such as information, technology, manpower, knowledge, management level, culture, etc. Among them, in the process of CSR synergy, the three most important resources are material resources, information and human resources. Therefore, the content of synergistic integration is concentrated in material resources, information resources and human resources.

The establishment of CSR synergy mechanism of transnational enterprises can maximize the sharing of resources (material resources, information and human resources). Therefore, the most important integration of CSR synergy of transnational enterprises is the sharing of resources. The premise of establishing the resource sharing mechanism is that the partners have the complementarity or heterogeneity of the resources or capabilities. The individual can obtain the available resources from the cooperative alliance to reduce the cost and increase the benefits, so that the overall income of the alliance is greater than the individual income of the alliance. And this is the fundamental motivation for the formation of the alliance. The sharing of resources in the CSR synergy mechanism of transnational enterprises enables the various entities in the system to directly use the resources they own, and indirectly use more non-self-resources, through the establishment of communication and cooperation mechanism, the reasonable allocation of resources can be implemented to maximize the value of the remaining resources.

3. Implementation of synergistic factor integration based on resource sharing

The implementation of synergistic factor integration, based on resource sharing, needs to focus on information processing, improve the openness of each subject's resources, and achieve efficient resource allocation. In other words, it is to establish a platform or organization that provides services for resource sharing and strive to solve the phenomenon of "information isolation", so that the CSR promotion of transnational corporations can achieve barrier-free flow across platforms, organizations and countries, and achieve efficient allocation and utilization of all resources of each subject.

In the specific implementation process, the biggest difficulty is the conflict between individual interests and overall interests, which is reflected in the contradiction between resource openness and information hiding (confidentiality). Since these resources belong to different entities, they are independent individuals, with their own activities, internal processes, and the confidentiality of maintaining their own business processes. However, the collaborative promotion mechanism based on the promotion of CSR is different from the general enterprise alliance and industrial cluster coordination, because there is no fundamental contradiction and competition between transnational corporations, host governments and society in the process of promoting CSR. Therefore, the sharing of resources is achievable, and each member can achieve resource sharing by coordinating based on the principle of factor cooperation. In the specific implementation, it can be achieved by: (1) establishing an information service platform or organization capable of providing information content and demand status, formulating cooperation goals based on consensus of all members; (2) formulating the grammar rules that information sharing must follow, and controlling the constraints of information transfer; (3) developing an indicator system for evaluating the degree of information sharing; (4)establishing an information feedback mechanism to continuously improve or motivate members' concerted actions through feedback.

5.2.5 Order Parameter Management - Common Value

1. The connotation of common value

Common value refers to the total of the beliefs, values, common goals, and a series of behaviors that are shared and consciously adhered to by all employees of the organization. It can provide inexhaustible motivation and support for the organization to complete a task and achieve organizational vision. However, the common value is not the result of spontaneous action. From the explicit formulation of the organization to the general recognition of the members, and to the conscious practice, it is necessary to guide and nurture the members at all levels and in all aspects of the organization. Once the common value is built, all members of the organization will have a mutual understanding of the organization's core values, strategies, goals, objectives, and guidelines, and fully understand the organization's situation and the position and function of their work in the overall situation. It promotes mutual trust and understanding among members. By making full communication, it helps form good interpersonal relationship, stimulate members' keen sense of mission and responsibility, and improve the coordination and control effect within the organization. The common value can form a unified thought, unified understanding and unified action within the organization, and make the organization work. Therefore, the common value is the core and cornerstone of organizational culture, the soul of the organization, and the spiritual pillar of the normal operation of the organization.

The necessity of common value lies in: (1) cohesion. Through the establishment of common beliefs and values within the organization, it creates an atmosphere of mutual trust, mutual understanding, solidarity and mutual assistance among members. At the same time, it can unify the ideological understanding of all members of the organization, enhance the cohesiveness of the organization, and provide inexhaustible motivation for the development of the organization; (2) guiding effect. Through the establishment of a common recognized code of conduct within the organization, unifying the behavior of the organization and guiding the behavior that shows the expectations of the organization. It is conducive to the unified command and regulation of the organization; (3) clear direction. Through the determination of the common goals within the organization, it is possible to clarify the direction of the organization's progress, so that all members of the organization have clear goals and direction of efforts and enhance the motivation of employees.

Through the construction of common values, the purpose of sustainable development of the organization can be achieved.

2. The order parameter of CSR synergy system- common value

There are two ways to generate order parameters: one is that the system spontaneously produces order parameters. The other is that people consciously choose and cultivate order parameters in the critical state of the system. This method exerts the subjective initiative of the person and makes the system develop in the desired direction. However, the choice of order parameters must be adhered to: (1) the principle of considering the situation, that is, the selected order parameter should match the environment and the development goals of each subject; (2) the principle of control, that is, the selected order parameter must be an element that the system can control and control; (3) the principle of collective identity, that is, the selected order parameter, as the guiding factor of the development direction of the management system, must have collective recognition, otherwise its function cannot be fully exerted.

This study considers that the common value is the order parameter of the CSR synergy management system of transnational enterprises. The reasons are twofold: First, the effective operation of the joint system of each entity depends on the synergy and coordination between the various subsystems within the system, which depends on whether the objectives of each subsystem are consistent with the overall objectives of the system, and the common value is the basis for promoting the social responsibility of transnational enterprises. The maximization of the comprehensive social value realized is the unification of individual goals and overall goals. Second, the common value is generated and developed based on considering the value pursuit of each subsystem. It is the fusion of the objectives of each subsystem and is widely accepted and recognized by various subsystems. It is a series of behaviors and common goals that each subsystem can consciously abide by, so it is instructive to the system.

Based on the analysis of the above two aspects, it can be seen that the common value is generated by the interaction between various subsystems within the system. It is a slow variable and plays a dominant role in the system mechanism. It enables multi-dimensional organization to change relationships within dimensions, between the dimensions, and between the organization and the environment, that is, from the previous independent relationship changes to mutual coordination. This change will also counteract the common value and promote its development and evolution. Therefore, the common value is the coordinated order parameter of the system of CSR synergy mechanism of transnational corporations.

The common value, which is taken as an objective parameter, is formed in the process of synergy between subsystems. When the common value of the system has not yet been formed, the subsystems cannot cooperate very well, because if there are multiple value objectives in the system, without a unified ideological understanding, the system lacks cohesion and each subsystem goes its own way. Only when each subsystem reaches a critical state, in which a cooperative relationship may occur, the system can form a cooperative relationship and act in concert, which leads to the emergence of order parameters and forms a common value within the system. Then, the common value guides and dominates the ideological concepts and values of each subsystem, and the behavioral norms that are recognized by each subsystem guide and control the work objectives of each subsystem at the management behavior level, thus ruling the evolution process of the system. After the formation of common values, the subsystems trust each other and share a keen sense of teamwork and ownership by sharing common values. When the internal and external environment in which the system is located is highly uncertain, even when the system changes rapidly and in order to formulate the corresponding countermeasures, the subjective initiative of each subject member and the strong sense of cooperation will still find solutions to the problem or act the desired behavior of the system in response to changing internal and external circumstances.

The formation of common values makes the objectives of each subsystem have a high sense of identity and commitment. After the formation of common values, the subsystems have a clearer goal toward the common mechanism of the system and mechanism. Through the decomposition of each layer, they are implemented to each member, thus clarifying the efforts of each member and enhancing their progress toward the goal of common struggle. It also enhances their potential to cooperate and coordinate with each other in the specific work of moving toward the goal of common struggle. The common value, through the internal coordination of the system, governs the good functioning of subsystems. The cooperation of the subsystems will also counteract the common value, and promote its development and evolution, that is, further consolidating and developing behavioral norms of membership identification system, and further strengthening the common goal.

5.2.6 Summary of Synergy Model

Under the guidance of the goal of CSR synergy, transnational corporations, host governments and societies have achieved the process synergy of the three, from the respective goal formulation to mechanism construction of economic responsibility, legal responsibility and moral responsibility. It has also realized the organization synergy, information synergy and resource synergy of the three. To achieve synergy effect, process synergy requires organization synergy, information synergy, and resource synergy to meet the needs of promotion in the form of dynamic interactions, as shown in Figure 5-2.

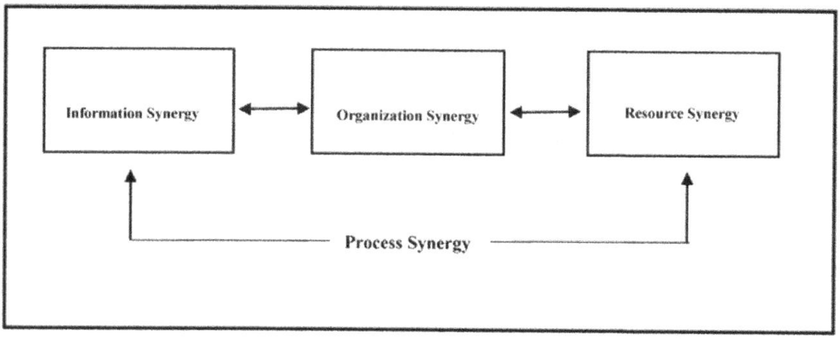

Figure 5-2 Information-organization-resource Synergy

The entire process of the CSR synergy implementation of transnational corporations reflects the process synergy. Transnational corporations, host governments, and societies, under the mechanism of synergistic promotion, analyze their actual conditions, clarify the goal synergy with the CSR coordination goals, and raise the social responsibility of transnational corporations to a strategic level, focusing on finding out inadequacies to clarify the direction in which CSR needs to be improved. Under the mechanism of synergistic advancement, the three will seek suitable collaborative entry points based on the collaborative feasibility analysis. For example, the incentives provided by the host government and society to the socially responsible transnational enterprises can improve the self-discipline of transnational enterprises. The three parties can integrate and link together, and under the orderly guidance of continuous development, continuously feedback and stimulate the system, and finally achieve the CSR goal of transnational enterprises, that is, to achieve the optimization (balance of stakeholders) of social responsibilities (economic responsibility, legal responsibility, environmental responsibility, moral responsibility and charitable responsibility), and the dynamic equilibrium development of economic, social and ecological benefits.

1. Organization synergy

The CSR organization synergy of transnational corporations emphasizes the inter-linkages among transnational enterprises, society and host governments, as well as between their respective sectors and members, to form a network-type collaborative organization that can operate in an orderly manner, focusing on integrity and structure. For example, the internal personnel and organizational synergy can make the members of the entire transnational enterprise deeply aware of the importance of responsibility, create a good social responsibility atmosphere, and implement them into daily business activities, improve employees' enthusiasm and the sense of belonging and accomplishment. Transnational corporations proactively publish social responsibility reports, publicize good responsibility behaviors, and the media simultaneously follow up and has become the magnifier of the voice of transnational corporations. Host governments and NGOs become social responsibility auditors and measurers, externalizing the assessment, making it fairer, and increasing its credibility and persuasiveness. It will also help the comparison between enterprises, so that transnational corporations can recognize their own situation and guide the direction of enterprise transformation.

2. Information synergy

The synergy promotion of transnational corporations, host governments, and society is the process of information transmission. Effective communication between the three is the basis for achieving synergy promotion. The information flow of transnational CSR has a wide range, including not only the information flow of transnational enterprises, such as rules and regulations information, organizational structure information, CSR performance information and report, but also the information flows from the needs, laws, supervision, evaluation and incentives of host governments and society. Therefore, synergy promotion requires these information flows to be delivered quickly, accurately and effectively among transnational corporations, host governments, and societies, making them a bridge between the two sides of CSR supply and each management party. Under the synergy of information, responsible transnational companies will gain a good reputation and establish a positive brand image. Consumers and shareholders will use the right to vote based on information. The host government judges the behavior of transnational corporations based on information, to decide to implement rewards or punishments.

3. Resource synergy

Resource synergy emphasizes the synergy of various material resources in addition to organization synergy (human resources) and information synergy (information resources). Specifically, there are internal capital flows, logistics, and other relevant infrastructure and material transfer provided by the host government and society. The external supervision, evaluation, incentives, pressures and other mechanisms of the host government and society directly affect the operation of transnational enterprises. The effects are more reflected in the long-term benefits of enterprises, including economic and social benefits. In this process, relevant resources transfer from outside the transnational corporation to internal. At the same time, during the process of CSR implementation of transnational corporations, part of internal resources is transferred to the outside, such as charitable donations and tax payments etc. This dynamic process of resource synergy will ultimately enable enterprises to gather more advantageous resources and form sustainable competitiveness.

5.3 CSR Evaluation Mechanism of Transnational Corporations in CMEC

5.3.1 Design Principles of CSR Evaluation Index System

From a macro perspective, the establishment of the evaluation system must have a theoretical basis. The composition of the evaluation system must have corresponding standards. On the micro level, the design of evaluation indicators should follow certain principles. The following principles should be followed in the selection of indicators, so that the social responsibility evaluation of transnational resource-oriented enterprises in the CMEC is as close as possible to objective facts.

This study follows the following principles in the design of the comprehensive evaluation index system for resource-oriented enterprises' social responsibility in CEMC:

1. The principle of combining comprehensiveness with systematicness

Comprehensiveness is a basic requirement for the social responsibility evaluation index system. Because it is necessary to reflect the comprehensiveness of the social responsibility index system of resource-oriented enterprises in CMEC, and the era, the selected indicators must be comprehensive. The principle of comprehensiveness is to consider the status and interrelationship of the various elements of the social responsibility of resource-oriented enterprises in CMEC. It is necessary to set corresponding indicators to fully reflect the social responsibility of enterprises. In short, the selected indicators should be as wide as possible, as many as possible, and as deep as possible, otherwise the results of the comprehensive evaluation will lose fairness.

Systematicity requires that indicators be classified according to certain methods, levels should be clearly defined, and all indicators have a certain degree of logic, so that the evaluation objectives and evaluation indicators are linked into an organic whole, rather than listing all the targets in a general way.

2. The principle of combining financial indicators with non-financial indicators

From the perspective of previous studies, business performance is often used as a measure of CSR. The most commonly used financial performance indicators in the company's business performance, so that the data on the accounting statements can be directly converted into financial ratios for evaluation. In the process of CSR comprehensive evaluation, the main part of economic responsibility often adopts financial indicators, and the same is true for transnational resource-oriented enterprises in CMEC. However, in view of the current situation and problems of the social responsibility performance of transnational resource-oriented enterprises in CMEC and the introduction of the indicator system of stakeholders in the index construction, a considerable number of non-financial indicators, such as the amount of safety investment and safety training people etc. These non-financial indicators are also more representative of the social responsibility of transnational resource-oriented enterprises, so both financial indicators and non-financial indicators are indispensable.

3. The principle of combining quantitative index with qualitative index

A quantitative indicator is an indicator that quantifies and represents the things or operations that are evaluated, usually in the form of currency, quantity, ratio, stage, etc. Commonly seen in transnational resource-oriented enterprises are: resource output, comprehensive energy consumption per 10,000 RMB of output value etc. Quantitative indicators are objective and scientific, and the selected indicators should be quantitative indicators as much as possible. But, not all indicators can be easily quantified. For example, in the comprehensive evaluation index system, there will be many indicators that are difficult to use numbers to express, such as whether to establish a CSR leadership organization, whether the company's homepage has a CSR column etc. These indicators, which are difficult to quantify, are called qualitative indicators. In the process of comprehensive evaluation of the social responsibility of transnational resource-oriented enterprises in CMEC, to ensure fairness and reasonableness, and not affect the overall situation, quantitative indicators should be avoided as much as possible. At the same time, the principle of combining qualitative indicators with quantitative indicators should be adopted, to reflect the comprehensive status of social responsibility of transnational resource-oriented enterprises in CMEC.

4. The principle of combing conciseness with importance

Since indicators are different from statistics and monitoring data, they must be processed to clearly reflect the problem. Conciseness means that indicators should simplify the information that reflects complex phenomena, so that people can understand and master them. The comprehensive evaluation index of social responsibility of transnational resource-oriented enterprises in CMEC must not only be concise, but also highlight the importance. Not only all the indicators are simple and clear, but also must be explained by words or by index weights and order to highlight important indicators. At the same time, the principle of importance requires that when conducting empirical research, the evaluation system should remove unimportant explanatory variables.

5. The principle of combining relevance with irrelevance

Relevant indicators indicate that the indicators at the next level must have a certain correlation with the indicators at the previous level. The indicators at the next level are generally the components of the indicators at the previous level; the irrelevance requires that the indicators at the same level remain linear as much as possible, especially it is necessary to avoid the complete linear correlation of the explanatory variables at the same level when doing the empirical test. Otherwise, it will lead to wrong measurement results, and make the evaluation system not evaluable.

6. The principle of combining comparability with controllability

The comparability indicator system cannot contain statistical indicators that are obviously prone. When using the evaluation index system for comparative analysis, it is often necessary to do horizontal and vertical sorting analysis. To make the evaluation results comparable, the selected CSR indicators should be generally applied among enterprises. The economic content, social impact, spatial scope, time range, calculation caliber, and calculation methods included in the indicators should be as consistent as possible. However, the controllability of indicators cannot be lost because of comparability. The principle of controllability requires that indicators that are beyond the control of the enterprise, Such as exchange rate fluctuations, major accidents and disasters etc.

7. The principle of combining innovation with operability

Innovation is generally the discovery of areas that have not yet been manipulated. Innovation is of foremost importance to the comprehensive evaluation of social responsibility indicators, but it is also very difficult. The introduction of ISO26000 promoted the concept of CSR to the social responsibility of any form of organization, and for the first time unified the definition of social responsibility globally, clarified the principle of social responsibility, determined the core theme of social responsibility, and described ways to integrate social responsibility into organizations, strategies and daily activities with the goal of sustainable development. Among them, the first theme of the seven core themes of ISO26000 is organizational governance, which can be said to be a prerequisite for realizing other social responsibility capabilities. This is a contribution and innovation of ISO26000 in social responsibility.

The innovation of indicators needs to combine theory with practice. Taking ISO26000 as an example, the innovation points in ISO26000 can be applied to the design of social responsibility indicators of transnational resource-oriented enterprises in CMEC. However, it should be combined with the actual situation of transnational resource-oriented enterprises operability should be considered. In short, operability should be the unity of innovation and achievability. It is necessary to fully consider the achievable degree of innovation indicators and their evaluation systems, not only to ensure innovation, but also to ensure that such innovation is conducive to promotion.

8. The principle of combining scientificity with evaluability

Scientific standards are expressed in four aspects, that is, to ensure the reliability, impartiality, objectivity and sustainability of the evaluation system. The evaluation system of the transnational resource-oriented enterprises of the CMEC constructed with evaluability requires not only the theoretical modelability, but also the practice and guiding practice of the transnational resource-oriented enterprises in CMEC. At any time, we must not pursue the science and discard the principle of evaluability.

The above eight principles reflect the 16 characteristics of evaluating the social responsibility of transnational resource-oriented enterprises in CMEC. The index system constructed according to these eight principles can not only reflect the contradiction and consistency of the social responsibility of the transnational resource-oriented enterprises in CMEC, but also reflect the relationship between the arduousness and achievability of the evaluation system. Therefore, the above eight principles have laid a scientific and solid foundation for the establishment of the social responsibility evaluation system for transnational resource-oriented enterprises in CMEC.

5.3.2 Evaluation Index Model

According to the system point of view, the improvement of the overall function of the system depends not only on the function of each subsystem, but also on the interaction between the subsystems. Therefore, the innovation of the evaluation mechanism of the CSR synergy of transnational resource-oriented enterprises lies in that it not only needs to evaluate the performance of each subsystem in the system, but also needs to grasp and understand the interaction and cooperation between subsystems. This part will focus on the four aspects of CSR synergy awareness, CSR communication, CSR resource sharing and cooperation capabilities.

The specific evaluation model is shown in Table 5-2. On the one side, the construction of evaluation mechanism has improved the system of CSR synergy mechanism of transnational resource-oriented enterprises. On the other side, the investigation of the interaction performance of transnational enterprises, host governments, society can provide guidance for further implementation of specific implementation measures and recommendations.

Table 5-2 Indicator Model of CSR Synergy Evaluation Mechanism of Transnational Enterprises: Based on Synergy Perspective Assessment

Primary Indicator	**Secondary Indicators**	**Operational Definitions of Secondary Indicators**		
		Transnational Corporation	**Host Government**	**Society**
W_1 Evaluation of the status quo of CSR fulfillment (or promotion) of transnational corporations: based on the consideration of the three entities	**U_1 CSR Awareness**	Is there a sense of compliance, whether to establish a sense of consciously fulfilling social responsibility, and whether to establish stakeholder awareness?	Whether to pay attention to the promotion of CSR, whether to establish awareness of promoting CSR, whether to focus on CSR promotion and education, and whether to focus on the concept and awareness of CSR?	Whether to pay attention to the promotion of CSR, whether to establish awareness of promoting CSR, whether to focus on CSR promotion and education, and whether to focus on the concept and awareness of CSR?

Primary Indicator	**Secondary Indicators**	**Operational Definitions of Secondary Indicators**		
		Transnational Corporation	**Host Government**	**Society**
	U_2 CSR Institutional Improvement	Whether to establish a CSR information disclosure mechanism, whether to establish a CSR indicator system, whether to establish a CSR assessment system, and whether to establish a department dedicated to CSR?	Is there a special law to promote CSR and continuous improvement, whether to establish a CSR indicator system, whether to set up a department dedicated to promoting CSR, whether to use administrative, auditing methods and certification methods to supervise the status of corporate responsibility?	Whether to establish a CSR indicator system, whether to establish corresponding industry standards, and whether to establish a department dedicated to promoting CSR?

Primary Indicator	**Secondary Indicators**	**Operational Definitions of Secondary Indicators**		
		Transnational Corporation	**Host Government**	**Society**
	U_3 **CSR Resource Guarantee**	Whether to provide special funds to support the implementation of CSR, whether to provide other material resources to support employees to fulfill their social responsibilities, and whether to deploy specialized personnel for CSR promotion?	Are there special funds and other material resources for supporting enterprises, governments, and society to implement or promote CSR, such as material support, human support, knowledge support, policy support, information support, etc., whether there are specialized personnel engaged in CSR work, whether to provide resources for research on CSR, whether to reward companies with good performance, such as government procurement behavior or direct economic incentives?	Are there special funds and other material resources to use to support or promote CSR for enterprises, society, such as material support, human support, knowledge support, policy support, etc., whether there are special personnel engaged in CSR work?

Primary Indicator	Secondary Indicators	Operational Definitions of Secondary Indicators		
		Transnational Corporation	**Host Government**	**Society**
	U_4 CSR Capacity Building	Whether to conduct CSR training for employees, and whether have successfully organized large-scale CSR activities or conferences?	What is the status of CSR law enforcement capabilities, the ability to organize large-scale CSR activities or meetings, and the ability to advance in international CSR?	Evaluation of the strength and influence of CSR supervision
W_2 Evaluation of the status quo of CSR synergy promotion in transnational enterprises: based on the consideration of the status quo of interaction and cooperation	**U_5 CSR Win-win Awareness**	Whether it has a global concept, whether to establish a "business-government", "enterprise-social organization", "enterprise-government-social organization" cooperation and win-win awareness?		
	U_6 CSR Communication Status	Whether to set up special intermediary agencies, technical intelligence agencies and well-functioning information exchange platform, and how to disclose resource information?		
	U_7 CSR Resource Sharing Status	Whether the circulation of people, information and resources is smooth, and whether the advantages of resources are complementary?		
	U_8 CSR Collaborative Ability	Whether it has successfully organized large-scale CSR activities and conferences with multiple parties, how much participation is involved, and whether each subject plays a significant role in activities and meetings?		

From the evaluation model constructed above, the evaluation of interactive performance is added on the basis of the original evaluation model, focusing on the aspects of synergy awareness, communication, and resource sharing and cooperation ability. Combined with the model of transnational CSR synergy mechanism, this model is a comprehensive evaluation and feedback on the collaborative mode and content, so it is a relatively complete and reasonable evaluation model.

In this summary, the three mechanisms of the transnational resource-oriented enterprise CSR promotion mechanism have been elaborated. The synergistic formation mechanism is the foundation, without which the synergistic mechanism will not be formed. Similarly, leaving the synergistic realization mechanism, the synergistic effect cannot be achieved. If there is no synergy evaluation mechanism, the overall operation status cannot be examined, and the system can be improved in time to ensure the realization of synergy. Therefore, the three of them together form an organic whole that works together to achieve synergy.

Chapter 6

Countermeasure Suggestions for CSR Synergy Promotion Mechanism of Transnational Resource-oriented Enterprise in CMEC

China and Mongolia are neighbors, with a border line of 4,710 kilometers. From the east to the west, there are 5 perennial open ports (Ceke, Ganqi Maodu, Erlianhaote, Takshken, and Zhuen Dabuk) and 13 seasonal open ports. The border line between Inner Mongolia (the neighboring province of China and Mongolia) and Mongolia is more than 3,000 kilometers long. Among them, the three most important coal ports, namely Ganqi Maodu, Ceke and Erlianhot, are in the Inner Mongolia. They have obvious complementary features and have always been in close exchanges. At the same time, Mongolia and Inner Mongolian have commonalities in language and belief and have unparalleled advantages. Since the establishment of the CMEC, Chinese enterprises have entered Mongolia, which is rich in mineral resources such as coal, copper and uranium. The economic and trade development of resource-oriented enterprises has not only boosted the Mongolian economy, but also accelerated the industrial upgrading of China.

However, for the resource-oriented enterprises in CMEC, their understanding of CSR is still not in place, and there are still many problems in the implementation of CSR. Based on the perspective of collaborative interaction, this part constructs the CSR synergy mechanism of transnational resource-oriented enterprises in CMEC. Its essence is to regard the issue of CSR as a global social problem, through the interaction and cooperation between transnational resource-oriented enterprises, host governments and the society, to achieve the harmony and win-win situation between China and Mongolia.

6.1 Countermeasures for transnational resource-oriented enterprises

1. Improve corporate governance structure

The design of governance structure of transnational resource-oriented enterprises can not only achieve the interests of enterprises and shareholders, but also consider the commitment issue of CSR. When making specific decisions, decision makers should also consider the relevant stakeholders, such as their employees and their regions, to fulfill their social responsibilities. First of all, the employee director and supervisor system are the embodiment of corporate responsibility in the corporate governance structure. Secondly, the responsibility of resource-oriented corporate social responsibility has a very important relationship with the independent director system.

2. Improve internal moral control mechanisms

Establishing a sound moral regulation mechanism within the enterprise is the main way of internal ethical regulation. First, the system introduces the mechanism of CSR ethics; secondly, to establish the corporate ethical decision-making mechanism; finally, to improve the corporate ethics training mechanism.

3. Meet the actual needs of key groups and stakeholders

In resource-oriented enterprises, when the selected public welfare undertakings are also concerned and valued by key groups and stakeholders, the support for social activities will reach its potential. For transnational resource-oriented enterprises, enterprises should satisfy and care about the working conditions, living conditions and psychological demands of the host country employees; for the external part of resource-oriented enterprises, the upstream and downstream industrial chains of the host country's energy industry, the interests of the host country residents, and the interests of the host government are the main targets to be maintained. Their interests must be satisfied. This is crucial for the smooth achievement of the production and operation objectives of resource-oriented enterprises.

4. Promote resource-oriented companies' response to CSR international initiatives or activities

Global agreements require transnational companies to shoulder more social responsibilities. However, the promotion and implementation of the current global agreement is unbalanced on a global scale. In particular, it is quite difficult for China's transnational enterprises to implement international high standards in developing countries and take part of their objective profits to carry out public welfare undertakings with little harvest in the short term. Therefore, the public should actively promote China's transnational resource-oriented enterprises' respond to international initiatives or activities of CSR and establish a good image and reputation in the host country and even the world.

5. Seize opportunity to promote host country support

China's resource-oriented enterprises should actively seek the support of non-governmental organizations and public institutions in the aiding countries or host countries. They should continue to give full play to their own advantages and adopt corresponding strategies to seek the support of these institutions. It is necessary to list the relevant themes of public welfare social undertakings that China's resource-oriented enterprises are prepared to implement, and to gain an in-depth understanding of the interests and experiences of non-governmental organizations and public institutions in aiding countries or host countries in supporting social activities, and to satisfy and cooperate with publicity and logistics, finally to achieve win-win.

6. Resource-oriented enterprises should actively participate in the economic construction and development of the host country

The purpose of resource-oriented enterprises to carry out production in different countries is undoubtedly to pursue profits. But at the same time, it is also responsible for the friendly exchanges with foreign countries of the Chinese nation and the implementation of the national resources strategy. It is an effective measure for resource-oriented enterprises to promote friendly exchanges with foreign countries and complete national strategies, such as helping residents to get rid of poverty, helping host countries to achieve economic growth, caring for vulnerable groups and solving employment problems. A good external socio-economic environment will help resource-oriented enterprises expand the host country and even the world market, improve the quality of employees and enhance the image and popularity of enterprises. If resource-oriented enterprises find ways suitable for the economic development of the host country according to their own competitive advantages, take an active part in solving the difficulties faced by the host country and realizing the goal of a harmonious world, resource-oriented enterprises are bound to complete the construction and practice of CSR from public benefit orientation to enterprise and social value maximization orientation.

Mongolia Metal Import and Export Co., Ltd. and China Nonferrous Metals NFC Co., Ltd. jointly implemented the "tumulteaobao" zinc mine project. The Chinese side owns 51% of the Xindu joint venture, and Mongolia holds 49% of the shares. Since the establishment of the Sino-Mongolian joint venture Xindu Company, it has operated according to law and paid taxes in accordance with the regulations, which has made great contributions to the development of Mongolia's economy, and has become a model for Sino-Mongolian mining cooperation and mutual benefit. Currently, the mine employs 215 Mongolian workers and 62 foreign experts. This has played a positive role in increasing local employment and driving the development of the local economy. Since the plant was put into production, the contribution rate to Mongolia's GDP has reached 2-2.5%. In addition, the Ulaanbaatar Railway Bureau and the "Tara Prague" coal mine in Sukhbaatar have seen a surge in sales and service revenues, which has also contributed to the increase in national budget revenue.

While emphasizing its own development, Xindu Company also actively participated in some local social welfare activities in Mongolia, to return to the local area and promote economic development in the region. The local government and the people also strongly support it.

The mine works with the province of Sukhbaatar to provide regular assistance to the education and health sectors. For example, the mine regularly pays tuition fees for 20 college students in Sukhbaatar province and has built a new optical fluoroscopy room for the provincial general hospital and renovated the ward. In addition, the mine invested 110 million to set up a 15 km optical cable between the mine site and the 40 counties of West Ural, connecting the mobile phone network of Mobicom and Skytel. In 2006, the 800th anniversary of the founding of the Great Mongolia, the company funded the local Nadam activities, donated 50,000 US dollars to build a Unity Parkin West Ural, and donated more than 110,000 US dollars to repair the road in West Ural (Gao, 2015).

In short, the performance of resource-oriented enterprises in the CMEC is not only related to the success or failure of their own operations, but also to the overall development of the industry and the overall image of the country. It's even related to that whether China's "win-win" opening-up strategy can be successfully implemented. Enterprises' taking the initiative to assume social responsibility is just the investment in the enterprise brand, reputation and social image. In a highly competitive international environment, enterprises must attach importance to and fulfill their social responsibilities to survive and develop.

6.2 Countermeasures for Host Governments to Strengthen CSR Implementation

1. Legal enforcement mechanism

The legal enforcement mechanism includes two basic aspects, one is law and; and the other is enforcement. Law, as one of the elements, as the name suggests, it is to improve the legislation to make CSR into a legal and standardized management system and guide the active and healthy development of transnational corporations. Relevant government agencies must strictly abide by the laws and regulations of CSR and carry out their work independently and responsibly under the authority of the law and the supervision of the public. At the same time, they must also increase the punishment for the violations of CSR of transnational corporations and must play a role in disciplining and changing.

First, establish and improve the legal system of mergers and acquisitions (M&A). There are two main forms of foreign investment by transnational corporations, namely, new construction; and mergers and acquisitions. Transnational mergers and acquisitions are most likely to produce monopoly behaviors, especially if the industry related to the national economy and people's livelihood is monopolized, it will cause the host country turbulence of social order. In contrast, the laws and regulations on the M&A behavior of transnational corporations only provide the principle provisions, which are too simple and general, and are not easy to operate. Therefore, the host country should establish a set of relatively complete review system of M&A of transnational corporations, which is suitable for the national conditions of the host country and impose strict restrictions on the M&A energy industry of transnational corporations.

Second, improve and perfect the supporting system related to anti-monopoly. The promulgation and implementation of anti-monopoly related laws and regulations plays a certain role in preventing and suppressing monopolistic behavior, protecting market fair competition, improving economic operation efficiency, safeguarding consumer interests and social public interests, and promoting the healthy development of the socialist market economy. However, anti-monopoly review is a work involving a wide range of topics and extremely complicated technology. It needs to be defined by relevant facts and data. These need to be explained in a detailed supporting system, otherwise it will be difficult to be convincing enough. Therefore, the host country should establish and improve the supporting system of the Anti-Monopoly Law as soon as possible.

Third, develop anti-commercial bribery and anti-money laundering regulations as soon as possible. Cases of bribery and money laundering by transnational corporations in the host country are not uncommon, but the host country has no relevant laws to restrict it, which results in the home country being able to impose penalties on transnational corporations, while the host country cannot, or they are less penalized. If the host country is a country where the market economy has just been established, it is crucial to maintain a fair market competition order. The corrosiveness of commercial bribery and money laundering to society cannot be underestimated. In the face of commercial bribery and money laundering by transnational corporations in the host country, the host country should eventually establish a set of anti-commercial bribery and anti-money laundering legal systems, and restrictive mechanisms to create a level playing field.

Forth, strengthen the legal construction of labor and consumer rights protection. Transnational corporations enjoy autonomy in terms of wage standards, and the host country's labor regulations have weaker restrictions on it. Therefore, in addition to incorporating transnational corporations into the scope of labor laws and regulations, it is also necessary to establish and improve labor arbitration systems, wage negotiation systems, and trade union organizations of transnational corporations, to protect the interests of labor. Consumer protection is somewhat like the protection of labor rights, and many host countries have less law to rely on. These laws are also weakly binding on transnational companies' infringement of consumer rights and may not even be treated fairly. Therefore, the host country should also incorporate the damage of consumer rights caused by the products of transnational companies into the relevant legal system, and deal with its infringement.

Fifth, improve environmental protection laws and regulations. The environmental protection laws and regulations system can be composed of the Constitution, the Basic Law, the Single Law, administrative regulations, departmental regulations, local regulations, environmental standards, and international environmental protection conventions. Many host countries' environmental legal systems are also becoming more and more perfect. However, the current Mongolian environmental policy legal system is still not suitable for its environmental protection work. There are many problems, such as few economic, technical and practical policies and lack of coordination among policies, soft environmental laws and regulations, weak operability, and too low penalty amount for illegal enterprises. As a result, some transnational resource-oriented enterprises make use of the conditions of imperfect environmental protection laws and regulations or low standards of the host country, fail to comply with laws, or transfer to the host country the industrial sectors with serious pollution. The host country should establish and improve environmental protection regulations that suit the national conditions as soon as possible, be in line with international standards, and strive to maximize the advantages of transnational resource-oriented enterprises to promote the development of the host economy.

2. Policy incentive mechanism

First, establish and publicize the concept of CSR. The host government plays a leading role in promoting the fulfillment of social responsibilities by transnational resource-oriented enterprises. While introducing foreign capital and promoting economic development, all levels of departments should firmly establish the concept of CSR and implement it into practical actions. Of course, the government also needs to publicize to transnational companies, and guide them to take the initiative to undertake social responsibilities, so that they can implement the concept of CSR into their daily business activities. In addition, the government should also play its own supervisory and public opinion-oriented functions, pay close attention to the social responsibility of each transnational company's host country, and make regular assessments to create an atmosphere and public opinion that seriously fulfills social responsibility. For transnational corporations that weaken social responsibility, they should make timely announcements, and even criticize or punish them according to the relevant laws and regulations of the host country.

Second, raise employees' awareness of safeguarding their rights. When a transnational company is in the host country, there will be behaviors that weaken employees' responsibilities, such as lowering salary standards, extending working hours and poor working environment. Employees often choose to be quiet about these, because they are worried about losing their jobs. To solve this problem, only the supervision effect of the government department is certainly not ideal. Employees need to enhance their awareness of rights protection. If a transnational corporation fails to perform its employee responsibilities in the host country, the employee shall take the initiative to report to the relevant authorities of the host country and, when necessary, take legal weapons to protect his rights and interests from infringement.

Third, stimulate government regulation. It is far from enough for the host government to supervise and punish transnational corporations. Incentives for government regulatory actions are also essential to ensure that transnational companies can fulfill their corporate social responsibility. The incentives for government regulatory behavior include both material and spiritual incentives. On the one side, the government should pay enough incentive fees to encourage regulators to take a more active regulatory attitude and increase the incentive for them to effectively supervise the violations of transnational corporations. On the other side, government agencies should give awards to law-enforcement agencies that enforce laws strictly and impartially, and honor and commend corresponding law-enforcement personnel, to reduce the possibility of government regulators colluding with transnational companies and accepting bribes.

Forth, give play to the role of NGOs and public opinion supervision. With the construction of the CMEC, the cooperation between China and Mongolia has become more and more in-depth, especially in the field of resources. There are more and more transnational resource-oriented enterprises in China and Mongolia. In the face of such a complex and volatile market, it is far from enough to rely on the power of the government to supervise the transnational resource-oriented enterprises to practice social responsibilities. It is also impossible to fully guarantee the comprehensive and effective government law enforcement. The host government should learn from the practices of developed countries, introduce more NGOs, and guide transnational resource-oriented enterprises to voluntarily assume CSR. By establishing CSR standards and improving CSR reporting systems, NGOs can disclose and evaluate the CSR fulfillment of transnational resource-oriented enterprises in a fair and equitable manner. Therefore, it is easier to be accepted by transnational resource-oriented enterprises and the public than direct government supervision.

To ensure the realization of the above-mentioned role of NGOs, the host government should first give the NGOs sufficient financial support to ensure the normal implementation of social responsibility promotion activities. It must have a policy orientation to support the development of NGOs. What's more, the government should avoid excessive administrative intervention to make NGOs operate independently and effectively.

Because of the characteristics of wide coverage, fast and far-reaching social influence, news and network media have gradually become the focus of supervision by public opinion. At present, the role of public opinion supervision of transnational corporations in the host society is still weak. On one side, it is because of the weak sense of public opinion supervision in the host country. On the other side, the channel for all sectors of society to play the role of supervision by public opinion is not yet clear. Therefore, the host country should create a relaxed political environment and legal atmosphere, vigorously promote the publicity work of public opinion supervision, encourage all sectors of society to supervise and report on the social responsibility of transnational corporations, and comprehensively promote the more and better fulfillment of social responsibilities by transnational corporations.

Bibliography

[1] Ansoff, H.I., Corporate Strategy, New York: McGraw-Hill, 1965.
[2] Amba-Rao S C. Multinational corporate social responsibility, ethics, interactions and Third World governments: An agenda for the 1990s. Journal of Business Ethics, 1993, 12(7):553-572.
[3] Bowen Howard R. Social responsibilities of the businessman. New York: Harper & Brothers,1953.
[4] Burt, R.S., Structural Holes. The Social Structure of Competition, Cambridge: Harvard University Press, 1992.
[5] Berry M A. Mastering Data Mining: The Art and Science of Customer Relationship Management. Industrial Management & Data Systems, 2000, 100(5): 245-246.
[6] Brown T J, Dacin P A. The company and the product: Corporate associations and consumer product responses. Journal of Marketing, 1997, 61(1): 68-84.
[7] Bennett J. MANAGING FINANCIAL RELATIONSHIPS IN CHALLENGING TIMES. Financial Executive, 2002(June).
[8] Clark David, An Approach to Corporate Social Responsibility, Stanford Law Review, 1979.
[9] Carroll, A.B., The Four Faces of Corporate Citizenship, Business and Society Review, 1998.
[10] Carroll Archie B. Corporate social responsibility: evolution of a definitional construct. Business and Society, 1999 ,38(3): 268-295.
[11] CED. Social responsibilities of business corporations. New York: Committee for Economic Development, 1971.
[12] Carroll A.B. The Pyramid of Corporate Social Responsibility. Toward the Moral Management of Organizational Stakeholders, Business Horizons, 1991.
[13] Davis K. Can Business Afford to Ignore Social Responsibilities? California Management Review, 1960, 2(3): 70-76.
[14] Donaldson T., Preston L.E., The Stakeholder Theory of the Corporation. Concepts, Evidence, and Implications, Academy of Management Review, 1995.
[15] Deckop J. R. & K. K. Merriman, The effects of CEO pay structure on corporate social performance, Journal of Management, 1999.
[16] Drucker Peter F. Mangement: tasks, responsibilities, practices. New York: HarperCollins, 1993 ed.: 39.
[17] Dill W A, Kelley D W, Fraser J C. Water- and land-use development and the aquatic environment - Problems and solutions. FAO Fisheries Technical Papers (FAO). No. 141. 1975.

[18] Friedman M., Capitalism and Freedom, Chicago University Press, 1962.
[19] Friedman M., The social responsibility of business is to increase its profit, New York Times Magazine, 1970.
[20] Frederick W.C., Corporate social responsibility in the Reagan era and beyond, California management review, 1983.
[21] Freeman C., The Economics of Industrial Innovation, the MIT Press, 1982.
[22] Freeman C., The national system of innovation in historical Perspective, Cambridge J. Econ, 1995.
[23] Howard R., Bowen, Social Responsibilities of the Businessman, New York Harper & Row, 1953.
[24] Jr Alfred Chandler D., Strategy and Structure. Chapters in the History of the American Industrial Enterprise, Washington, D.C.: Beard Books, 2003.
[25] John R. Baldwin, Richard E., Caves, Foreign Multinational Enterprises and Merger Activity in Canada, University of Calgary Press, 1998.
[26] Jarillof J.C., On the Strategic Networks, Strategic Management Journal, 1988.
[27] Koester, Wolfgang. Cross-Border Conflagration, AFP Exchange, 2010.
[28] Levitt T. The dangers of social responsibility. Harvard Business Review, 1958, (9-10): 41-45.
[29] Laughlin J L, Ahsan M B. A Strategic Model for Multinational Corporation Social Responsibility in the Third World. Journal of International Marketing, 1994, 2(3): 101-115.
[30] Levis J. Adoption of corporate social responsibility codes by multinational companies. Journal of Asian Economics, 2006, 17(1): 50-55.
[31] Moore G. Corporate Social and Financial Performance: An Investigation in the U.K. Supermarket Industry. Journal of Business Ethics, 2001, 34(3/4): 299-315.
[32] Matten D., J. Moon. A Conceptual Framework for Understanding CSR, In A. Habisch, J. Jonker, M. Wegner and R. Schmidpeter (eds.), Corporate Social Responsibility Across Europe (Springer, Berlin) .
[33] Marrewijk M V. Concepts and Definitions of CSR and Corporate Sustainability: Between Agency and Communion. Journal of Business Ethics, 2003, 44(2/3): 95-105.
[34] Marens R. Recovering the past: reviving the legacy of the early scholars of corporate social responsibility. Journal of Management History, 2008, 14(1): 55-72.
[35] Oliver Sheldon, The Philosophy of Management, 1924.
[36] Prahalad C.K., Hamel G., The Core Competence of the Corporation, Harvard Business Review, 1990.

[37] Robbins Stephen P, Mary Coultar. Management. Prentice Hall, 1996.
[38] Rondinelli D A. Multinational Strategic Alliances and Acquisitions in Central and Eastern Europe: Partnerships in Privatization. The Academy of Management Executive (1993-2005), 2000, 14(4): 85-98.
[39] Rodriguez P, Siegel D S, Hillman A, et al. Three Lenses on the Multinational Enterprise: Politics, Corruption, and Corporate Social Responsibility. Journal of International Business Studies, 2006, 37(6): 733-746.
[40] Sheldon Oliver. The social responsibility of management, the philosophy of management. London: Sir Isaac Pitman and Sons Ltd, 1924.
[41] Spencer B A, G S Taylor. A within and between analysis of the relationship between corporate social responsibility and financial performance. Akron business and economic review, 1987.
[42] Stanwick P. A., Stankwick S.D., The Relation between Corporate Social Performance and Organizational Size, Financial Performance, and Environmental Performance: an Empirical examination, Journal of Business Ethics, 1998.
[43] Schuler D. A., Cording M. A., Corporate social performance-corporate financial performance behavioral model for consumers，Academy of Management Review，2006.
[44] Stoll M L. Backlash Hits Business Ethics: Finding Effective Strategies for Communicating the Importance of Corporate Social Responsibility[J]. Journal of Business Ethics, 2008, 78(1-2):17-24.
[45]The World Bank. Corporate social responsibility practice, public sector roles in strengthening corporate social responsibility: taking stock.2004:3.
[46]Van BH, An employee-centered model of corporate social performance, Business Ethics Quarterly, 2005.Chinese Part
[47]阿尔温·托夫勒(Alvin Toffler).《第三次浪潮》，朱志众译，北京三联书店，1983 年.
[48]边一，王浦. 我国矿业企业对外投资中的社会责任问题研究[J]. 中国人口·资源与环境, 2014, v.24;No.163(S1):444-447.
[49]陈宏辉，贾生华. 企业社会责任观的演进与发展:基于综合性社会契约的理解[J]. 中国工业经济, 2003(12):85-92.
[50]戴志强，从事件看企业社会责任[J]，企业管理，2007（3）：P15
[51]高潮.蒙古打造“草原之路”走廊对接中国“一带一路”战略[J].中国对外贸易,2015(10):72-73.
[52]哈罗德•孔茨,海因茨•韦里克.《管理学》，经济科学出版社，2003.
[53]胡大立,《企业竞争力决定因素及其形成机理分析》，北京经济管理版社，2004 年.
[54]韩梅. “一带一路”与蒙古国“草原之路”对接框架下的能矿产业合作研究[D]. 2017.

[55]胡格吉勒图. 蒙古国矿产资源开发现状及挑战因素分析[J]. 东北亚学刊, 2017(3):26-33.
[56]黄凌云, 郑淑芳, 王珏. “一带一路”背景下对外投资企业的合作共赢机制研究——基于社会责任视角[J]. 管理评论, 2018, 30(2):172-182.
[57]贾晓晴. 资源型企业与地方政府的关系研究——以辽河油田和盘锦市为例[D]. 中国地质大学(北京), 2008.
[58]吉海涛. 资源型企业生态责任的利益相关者协同作用分析[J]. 南京理工大学学报(社会科学版), 2009, 22(1):97-100.
[59]姜鸿, 张艺影. FTA 框架下中蒙矿产资源合作模式[J]. 东北亚论坛, 2012, 21(1):20-27.
[60]喆儒. 中国企业跨国经营的社会责任研究[J]. 北京金融评论, 2015(2):76-85.
[61]克雷格·史密斯.《新的企业慈善行为》,《哈佛商业评论》1994 年第 5 期.
[62]刘俊海,《企业的社会责任》, 法律出版社, 1999 年.
[63]卢代富,《企业社会责任的经济学和法学分析》,北京法律出版社,2002 年.
[64]刘长喜.利益相关者、社会契约与企业社会责任[D]. 复旦大学, 2005.
[65]刘豫杰. 新常态下促进中蒙俄经济走廊建设研究——探索内蒙古自治区沿边贸易合作开放机制创新[J]. 前沿, 2016(3):38-44.
[66]迈克尔·波特(Michael E. Porter),《国家竞争优势》, 北京中信出版社, 2003 年.
[67]迈克尔·波特(Michael E. Porter)、马克·克雷默(Mark R. Kramer).《企业慈善事业的竞争优势》,《哈佛商业评论》2003 年第 2 期.
[68]迈克尔·波特(Michael E. Porter),《竞争战略》, 陈小悦译,华夏出版社, 2005 年.
[69]迈克尔·波特(Michael E. Porter)、克拉斯·范德林德(Claas van der Linde).《环保与竞争力:对峙的终结》,《哈佛商业评论》2006 年第 1 期.
[70]马国君. 中蒙矿产资源合作开发研究[D]. 内蒙古大学, 2007.
[71]迈克尔•帕金.《微观经济学(第 8 版)》张军等译, 人民邮电出版社, 2013.
[72]朴光姬. 中国与朝鲜经贸关系转型中的困境及对策[J]. 东北亚论坛, 2012, 21(3):44-53.
[73]曲福田,《资源经济学》, 中国农业出版社, 2001 年.
[74]邱明星. 从企业自身视角看企业社会责任对其盈利目标的影响[J]. 华东经济管理, 2008, 22(1):120-124.
[75]任巧巧. 企业的社会责任与企业声誉[J]. 经济管理, 2005(19):16-20.
[76]斯蒂芬·夏彼洛,《永续创新》, 高颖、陈可等译, 新北京电子工业出版社, 2003 年.

[77]沈艺峰、沈洪涛,《企业社会责任思想:起源与演变》，上海人民出版社，2007 年.
[78]孙瑾瑾, 李娟. “中蒙俄经济走廊”建设背景下中蒙贸易合作发展的机遇与对策[J]. 知与行, 2015(5):31-35.
[79]沈铭辉, 张中元. 中国境外经贸合作区:“一带一路”上的产能合作平台[J]. 新视野, 2016(3):110-115.
[80]陶克涛,《竞争战略论》，中国财政经济出版社，2010 年.
[81]吴福顺, 管竹笋, 郑若娟. 2007 中国责任消费调查报告[J]. WTO 经济导刊, 2008(4):42-45.
[82]王赵宾. 中蒙煤炭贸易困局[J]. 能源, 2013(1):70-72.
[83]王明亮. 基于博弈论的企业社会责任形成机理研究[J]. 工业技术经济, 2013(2):13-18.
[84]徐淳厚. 试论商业企业的社会责任[J]. 经济纵横, 1987(9):44-47.
[85]谢文心.“一带一路”建设下中蒙经贸合作与发展[J].经济问题,2017(02):14-18.
[86]姚愉芳、贺菊煌,《中国经济增长与可持续发展—理论、模型与应用》, 社会科学文献出版社,1998 年.
[87]易开刚. 民营企业社会责任:内涵、机制与对策——基于竞争力的视角[J]. 经济理论与经济管理, 2006, V(11):65-69.
[88]姚海华. 东北亚一体化视角下的中蒙贸易关系演化分析[J]. 国际贸易问题, 2010(8):47-52.
[89]于洪洋, 欧德卡, 巴殿君. 试论“中蒙俄经济走廊”的基础与障碍[J]. 东北亚论坛, 2015(1):96-106.
[90]袁楚风. "一带一路"战略下中国对外投资企业社会责任分析[J]. 温州大学学报(社会科学版), 2018(2):074-79.
[91]周三多、邹统钎,《战略管理思想史》，复旦大学出版社, 2002 年.
[92]朱迪·丽丝,《自然资源:分配、经济学与政策》，商务印书馆，2002 年.
[93]张秀杰. 蒙古经济发展对中蒙经贸合作的影响[J]. 俄罗斯中亚东欧市场, 2005(11):33-37.
[94]张秀杰. 蒙古矿产资源开发状况及中蒙资源合作前景[J]. 东北亚论坛, 2005, 14(4):13-16.
[95]周祖城. 企业社会责任:视角、形式与内涵[J]. 理论导刊, 2005(2):58-61.
[96]张涛. 蒙古新《矿产法》对我国投资者的影响分析[J]. 中国国土资源经济, 2007, 20(11).
[97]中国煤炭学会,《煤炭生产一线技术创新与实践》, 煤炭工业出版社，2008 年.
[98]周祖城,《企业伦理学》，清华大学出版社，2009 年.

[99]周晨. 中国上市公司企业社会责任的竞争优势战略属性研究——来自沪深两市 731 家上市公司经验证据[J]. 华东经济管理, 2010, 24(4):111-117.
[100]张博. 企业社会责任与财务管理目标的重新定位——基于利益相关者理论视角[J]. 商业经济研究, 2011(18):83-84.
[101]郑淑伟. 中蒙两国煤炭贸易未来发展的思考[J]. 内蒙古民族大学学报（社会科学版）, 2013, 39(1):88-90.
[102]张婧. 山西煤炭企业社会责任评价问题研究[D]. 山西财经大学, 2014.

Index

D

E

F

G

H

I

J

K

L

M

T

U

V

W

Z

About the Authors

Eerdun Taoketao, male of Mongolian nationality, born on September 25, 1963, received a bachelor's degree in economics in Inner Mongolia University of Finance and Economics in July 1985, a master's degree in economics in Renmin University of China in July 2000, and a doctor's degree in management in Renmin University of China in July 2005.

Eerdun Taoketao is the director of the Department of Graduate Education and Discipline Planning and Construction, Inner Mongolia University of Finance and Economics, second-grade professor, visiting research fellow of Hitotsubashi University, and concurrently tutor of doctoral degree candidates in the Institute of Finance and Economics of Mongolia, ERDEM University, Ulaanbaatar, Mongolia. He was listed among young and middle-aged outstanding contributors to the Inner Mongolia Autonomous Region in 2012, and an outstanding educator in the Inner Mongolia Autonomous Region in 2012 and was named as an expert receiving special government allowance from the State Council in 2016.

He majors in the theory of corporate social responsibility, strategic management, industrial innovation and economic development. He presided over and participated in more than 30 programs in the National Social Science Fund and other funds, published more than 40 papers and 15 monographs and textbooks. He won a second prize in the State-level Teaching Award, two first prizes in the Teaching Award of the Inner Mongolia Autonomous Region, and two first prizes and two second prizes of Social Sciences Award of the Inner Mongolia Autonomous Region. He is member of China Society of Soft Sciences, vice chairman of Economic Professional Committee of Minority Areas of China Association of Regional Economies, member of Preparatory Branch of the China Society of Ethnic Education, member of Inner

Mongolia Overseas Friendship Association and senior management consultant of several enterprises.

Zhang Zhe, female of Mongolian nationality, born on October 4, 1977, received a bachelor's degree in economics in Inner Mongolia University of Finance and Economics in July 2000, a master's degree in economics in Inner Mongolia University of Technology in July 2006, and a doctor's degree in management in Central University of Finance and Economics in July 2017.

She majors in the theory of corporate social responsibility, strategic management, enterprise technology innovation. She presided over and participated in more than 10 programs in the National Social Science Fund and other funds, published more than 12 papers.

Wang Gang, male of Han nationality, born on May 29, 1982, is the doctoral candidate at Central University of Finance and Economics and also the lecturer of Inner Mongolia University of Finance and Economics. He specialized in the study on corporate social responsibility, strategic management and entrepreneur management, and has published two textbooks and many papers.

Wei Lisi, female of Mongolian nationality, born on June23, 1987, is the doctoral candidate at Mongolian University of Finance and Economics. Published paper Research on Environmental Accounting and Corporate Social Responsibility Under the Background of 'The Belt and Road' etc.

Made in the USA
Monee, IL
05 November 2026

67808619R00125